THE

HISTORY AND ANTIQUITIES

OF THE

COLLEGIATE

Church of Tamworth,

IN THE COUNTY OF STAFFORD.

BY

CHARLES FERRERS R. PALMER, O.P.

Tamworth:

J. THOMPSON, BOOKSELLER, MARKET STREET.

LONDON: SIMPKIN, MARSHALL, AND CO.

1871.

TAMWORTH :

J. THOMPSON, PRINTER, MARKET STREET.

To the
Inhabitants of Tamworth,
Who regard with Affectionate Reverence

Their venerable Parish Church,

This Record
of the

Piety and Devotion of their Forefathers

is

Respectfully Dedicated.

List of Subscribers.

Rawle, Rev. R., the Vicarage, Tamworth, *two copies, toned paper*

Repington, C. H. W. A'Court, Esq., 29, Lowndes St., S.W., *two copies, toned paper*

Arnold, W. Esq., Tamworth, *two copies, toned paper*

Arnold, Joseph, Esq., the Leys, Tamworth, *toned paper*

Argyle, T., Esq., Tamworth, *toned paper*

Allkins, Mr., Market Street, *toned paper*

Art Library, South Kensington Museum, *two copies (one toned paper)*

Bramall, G. H., Esq., Chester, *toned paper*

Bramall, Henry, Esq., Notting Hill, London, *toned paper*

Baldwin, Mr., Tamworth

Buckler, Charles Alban, Esq., 6, Hereford Sq., Brompton, S.W., *toned paper*

Bracebridge, C. H., Esq., Atherstone, *toned paper*

Browne, Rev. A., Drayton Bassett, *toned paper*

Bradbury, Mr. John, Tamworth

Brown, R., Esq., Wigginton House, *toned paper*

Clarson, Mr. C., Tamworth, *toned paper*   [*paper)*

Cooke, T. Esq., Tamworth Castle, *two copies (one toned*

Cowpland, Rev. R., Weeford, *toned paper*

Clarson, Mr. Abel, Tamworth, *toned paper*

Clarson, Mr. Arthur A., Tamworth, *toned paper*

Canning, Charles, Esq., Glascote, *toned paper*

Cranbrook, Rev. J., Tamworth

Calloway, E., Esq., Tamworth, *toned paper*

Davis, Rev. J. W., the Grammar School, *toned paper*

Dean, Mr. J., Tamworth

Eaton, Miss, Tamworth, *toned paper*

Estcourt, Very Rev. E. Canon, Bishop's House, Birmingham,
    toned paper

Freer, Rev. W. H., Seckington

Featherstone, John, Esq., High St., Warwick, *toned paper*

Gray, Mrs., the Moat House, *toned paper*

Grover, Rev. T. C., Wilnecote

Harding, Miss, Tamworth, *toned paper*

Hollins, R. A., Esq., Mansfield

Hulland, Mr., Tamworth, *toned paper*

Hughes, Rev. T. M., Clifton Campville

Hamel, E. D., Esq., Tamworth, *toned paper*

Hodge, Rev. H. V., Middleton, *toned paper*

Inge, Rev. G., Thorpe Constantine, *two copies, toned paper*

Jennings, J. L., Esq., Tamworth, *toned paper*

Lloyd, Miss, Rhyl, *toned paper*

Lloyd, Rev. F. Ll., Aldworth, *toned paper*

Lomax, Mr. T. G., Lichfield, *two copies (one toned paper)*

Mayou, J. W., Esq., Bonehill, *toned paper*

Morgan, Mr., Market Street, *toned paper*

Moon, R., Esq., Wigginton Lodge, *toned paper*

Mayou, Rev. B., Baddesley, *toned paper*   [*paper*

Millar, Rev. J. O., L.L.D., Cirencester, *two copies toned*

Martin, John, Esq., Ledbury Hall, *toned paper*

Mould, Rev. J., Oakham, *toned paper*

Madan, Rev. Nigel, Polesworth, *toned paper*

Mitchell, Mr. A., Tamworth

Nield, Rev. C. H., Tamworth

Northcote, Very Rev. J. S., D.D., S. Mary's College, Oscott

Peel, J., Esq., M.P., Middleton Hall, *toned paper*

Peel, Miss, Harrow Lands, Dorking

Price, T. E., Esq., Dosthill, *toned paper*

Pipe, Miss, Tamworth, *toned paper*

Purcell, Rev. U. W., Wigginton Vicarage, *toned paper*

Palmer, Shirley F., Esq., Birmingham, *two copies (one toned*
Rawlins, Rev. F., Clifton, *toned paper*   [*paper)*
Ruffe, F., Esq., Tamworth, *toned paper*
Starkey, Mr. C., Tamworth
Sculthorpe, A. M., Esq., Tamworth, *toned paper*
Stewart, Captain, Chester Street, Edinburgh, *toned paper*
Tempest Mr. W., Tamworth, *toned paper*
Tanner, Rev. R. H., Fazeley Vicarage, *toned paper*
Tamworth Natural History, Geological, and Antiquarian
      Society, *toned paper*   [*paper*
Turner, J., Esq., Horninglow St., Burton-on-Trent, *toned*
Thompson, Rev. J., Blackheath, *two copies, toned paper*
Willington, F., Esq., Tamworth, *two copies, toned paper*
Willington, Rev. F., Worton Rectory, Oxfordshire, *toned*
Willington, Rev. J. R., Torquay, *toned paper*   [*paper*
Willington, Rev. H. E., London, *toned paper*
Wolferstan, F. S. P., Esq., Statfold Hall, *toned paper*
Wileman, Mr., Market Street, *toned paper*
Woody, R. I., Esq., the Moat House, *toned paper*
Williams, Rev. W. B., Tamworth, *toned paper*
Welchman, Mrs. C. E., Lichfield

PREFACE.

_____

IT is now more than a quarter of a century since we wrote the "HISTORY OF THE TOWN AND CASTLE OF TAMWORTH." It was gathered in the greatest measure from printed works. Being thus taken from very limited sources of knowledge the history in many points was necessarily broken, incomplete, uncertain, and even faulty in some details. But when larger and brighter prospects of research dawned upon us and the grand archives of the kingdom and private collections of manuscripts were opened to our use, we betook ourselves to enlarge, to correct, and to mould again. And we succeeded even beyond our highest hopes in throwing new and important lights upon our subject.

We now bring out some part of our later and better labours,

—————— wrestling with Time

To win the prize and make the Past be Present.

The History of the COLLEGIATE CHURCH OF ST. EDITH OF TAMWORTH has hitherto been very imperfectly known, being wrapped in doubts and difficulties and poor in detail. But now it comes forth in certainty and full of historical and antiquarian matter. The time of the first foundation of the College is fixed. The changing fortunes of the Church are traced through six hundred years. The Life of the Patron Saint is pourtrayed. The obituary and other endowments are recorded. The earliest provision for public education in the town comes into view. The Fasti of the Church show names of ecclesiastical dignitaries and statesmen who shed a lustre or left a mark or blot upon their age. The dissolution of the College is given at length The ancient fabric of the Church is described as far as records and architectural relics point out the details. And numerous incidents are narrated which interest at once the historian, the antiquarian, and the general reader. Very few Parish Churches in England have their histories so fully written as the one at Tamworth herein possesses.

Such are the leading features of the work which we give to the public. The documents of the Public Record Office, the manuscripts of the British Museum, and the records of the old Corporation of Tamworth have been freely searched. Much too has been gleaned from the Registers and other documents of the Parish, and from deeds and papers in private hands and chiefly those of the ancient Castle of this town. These are the main but not sole sources whence we have drawn a fresh addition to Archæology.

We must not forbear to acknowledge that we owe very much in our researches to many gentlemen of Tamworth and its neighbourhood, and more particularly to Rev. Edward Harston late Vicar of the Church, to Francis Willington, Esq., and to John Francis Woody, Esq., of the Moat House. After nearly twenty years have glided by, the fruits of their kindness spring forth in the present pages.

London : September, 1871.

Contents.

—§—

Appendix.

THE

HISTORY AND ANTIQUITIES,

&c.

ℋISTORY AND ᴀNTIQUITIES, &c.

CHAPTER I.

THE ANGLO-SAXON CHURCH.

IN the year 597 Christianity was planted amongst the Anglo-Saxons of this country. Within eighty-five years it became fixed throughout the length and breadth of the land held by the worshippers of Woden and Thor, whose altars crumbled under the power of the new teaching. Mercia, the largest of the Anglo-Saxon kingdoms, received the spreading faith in 655, and was put under the spiritual charge of a bishop whose rule at first reached even to the uttermost bounds of Northumbria. Ceadda (St. Chad), fifth bishop of the Mercians, fixed his See in the year 667 within seven miles of Tamworth, at Lichfield, that "Field of Dead Bodies," where unnumbered martyrs had shed their blood for Christ in the Dioclesian persecution. This See was raised into an archbishopric in 785, with six suffragans under it; but in 803 it was brought down to its first state, and ranked again as a member of the Province of Canterbury.

There must have been a church at Tamworth within a hundred years after Christianity was thus brought into the middle of England. In those early times there was no settled place of government. The government went with the person of the king and with his witan or council, and the king dwelt where need or custom or pleasure called him. So palaces were scattered up and down through all the country; and Tamworth was one of the most celebrated of those royal haunts. Here the Mercian kings often took up their quarters, chiefly at the high festivals of Christmas and Easter; and here Offa, Coenwulf, Berhtwulf, and Burghred, granted many charters to religious bodies between the years 781 and 857. Amongst those who waited on the king and his court, or formed his witan, were bishops and other ecclesiastics, who must have had a building at Tamworth for religious worship adorned with all due pomp. It is even likely that *Eadgar presbiter* and *Uuigberht presbiter*, who witnessed one of Coenwulf's charters in 814, and *Aetheluulf presbiter*, who signed one of Berhtwulf's in 845, were priests here, the documents bearing dates at this town.

The first Church cannot have escaped being destroyed when the Danes overran the country, in the year 874 and razed Tamworth to the ground. The town lay in ruins till Ethelfled, "Lady of the Mercians," lion-hearted daughter of the great Alfred, restored the country step by step, overcoming the Danes in many a battle, and forcing them to her rule. Early in the summer of 913 she marched with all the Mercians to Tamworth, and built the burh; the Saxon Chronicle says, "by the help of God," and thus marks how weighty was the deed. Ethelfled died, June 13th 918 at Tamworth. Here too Athelstan bestowed on Sihtric the hand of her to whom the Church was afterwards dedicated.

CHAPTER II.

SAINT EDITH, VIRGIN.

SIHTRIC was a Danish sea-king, as famous and as fierce as his father Ivar in pillaging and laying waste the English coasts. He became one of the many kings whom the ever-restless Danes, from time to time, set up in Northumbria. When the English seemed to be weakened by the death of Edward the Elder, in the year 924, and by the succession of Athelstan to the throne, he suddenly burst into their country with a ruthless army, but met with such a defeat in his own domains from Athelstan that he sued for peace. Athelstan made a treaty with him. Sihtric agreed to become a Christian, for his wife was now dead, and he was smitten with the charms of Athelstan's sister Eadgith, a younger daughter of Edward the Elder. Athelstan and Sihtric came together at Tamworth, Jan. 30th 925, and here with great honour and glory "Æthelstan his sweostor him forgeaf,"—Athelstan gave him his sister.

It was deemed unseemly for an English princess, daughter and sister of kings, to sink down in rank to the level of the wife of a Danish Jarl. So Athelstan gave back the country between the Tees and the Frith of Forth to Sihtric, and let him govern it with all royal power. But the Dane could not bear the curb. In a few months he fell back into paganism and broke out against Athelstan, but perished wretchedly in 926 before the forces of Athelstan reached him. His sons fled, Godefrid into Scotland, and Olaf or Anlaf into Ireland. Both strove in vain to get their father's kingdom. Anlaf was utterly overthrown in the great battle of Brunansburh, and never dared to appear again whilst Athelstan was alive. Godefrid became a roving sea-king.

No hearty bond of feeling could have knit together the young Christian maiden princess and the pagan sea-robber full of crimes, who by the murder of his brother Neil even had the blood-stain of Cain upon his brow. Eadgith was an offering for the peace and welfare of her country. But the ceremony undergone at Tamworth must have been rather the fore-giving, or solemn espousals, than the last marriage rite. The old annalists as good as say that Eadgith never joined her husband; and it is borne out in the records of this town, wherein she is always mentioned as a virgin-saint. She soon plighted her troth to Heaven in a monastery, where she passed a life so strict and good, in prayer, fasting, watchings and alms-deeds, that she won great fame for holiness; and when it came to be commonly believed, after she died, that miracles were wrought through her pleadings, the local bishops sanctioned that faith and enrolled her name in the catalogue of the Saints.

The Acts, or Life, of St. Eadgith cannot now be found. A few particulars concerning her may be gleaned in the great harvest of English history. In the *Liber de Hyda* which carries the history of the Abbey of Hyde in Hampshire down to the year 1023, it is said that Edward the Elder "duas habuit uxores, et unam concubinam. Ex concubinâ, Egwynna nomine, genuit Athelstanum, qui post ipsum regnavit, et Elfredum, et Edgytham, quæ nupsit Sirichio regi Northanhymbrorum, quæ requiescit Tamworthæ, et pro sanctâ colitur." The fair title of consort or queen is due to Egwynna: she was slighted by some of the old annalists, because she was not of a royal race though of noble descent. Hugo Candidus or Hugh White, a monk of Peterborough who flourished about the year 1216, speaking of the burial-places of English Saints says "& in Thamwrthe sancta Edgitha." Roger Wendover of St. Alban's Abbey who died in 1237 writes more fully thus: " Anno Domini DCCCCXXV. Ethelstanus, rex Anglorum, Eathgitam, sororem suam, Sithrico Danicâ natione progenito, Northanhumbrorum regi, matrimonio honorifice copulavit; qui, ob amorem virginis paganismum relinquens, fidem Christi suscepit, sed non multo post beatam virginem repudians, ac Christianitatem abjiciens, idolorum culturam restauravit, et post modicum temporis apostatus vitam miserabiliter terminavit. Sancta itaque puella, virginitate sibi reservatâ, apud Pollesberiam, in jejuniis et vigiliis, in orationibus et in eleemosynarum studiis, usque ad finem vitæ suæ bonis pollens operibus persever-avit; transiit autem, post laudabilis vitæ cursum, ex hoc mundo ibidem idibus Julii, ubi usque hodie divina miracula non desinunt celebrari." Matthew of Westminster and Richard of Cirencester both follow Wendover; whilst Thomas Rudborne a monk of Winchester, in the middle of the fifteenth century has taken the *Liber de Hyda* for his text when he writes, "Genuit etiam iste Edwardus ex Egwynnâ filiam nomine Edgytham; quæ nupsit Sirichio Comiti Northanhumbrorum; quæ & requiescit apud Tanwitham, & pro Sanctâ colitur." Leland in his Collectanea notes *E vita S. Edithæ* [de Wilton] *ab incerto autore edita,* "Eadgitha, Edgari germana, abbas de Tameworth, in provinciâ Stafordensi." Later historians give no good help, except perhaps Speed who in his *History of Great Britaine* says, but without giving good authority, that St. Eadgith "obtained of her brother's gift, the Castell of *Tamworth*, in the County of *Warwicke*, where she began a Monastery of Nunnes, and therein liued, died,

and was interred, and both the Monastery and
Body afterwards was remoued from thence vnto
Pollesworth." Polesworth, four miles distant,
was part of the ancient demesnes of the Castle.

After thus founding a Monastery at Tamworth
and ruling it as Abbess, St. Eadgith died, probably
about the year 960, when she was about sixty
years old. Some trustless Scotch historians, who
call her Beatrice and say that she was convicted
of poisoning her husband, place her death about
980 at Polesworth. Her *deposition* or burial
took place July 15th, and that day was fixed for
her yearly festival. In after-times the name
Eadgith, losing its Teutonic roughness, was at-
tuned to the Latin tongue and softened into
Editha or Edith. The history of her monastery
is unknown, save that soon after the Conquest
the Nuns must have removed to Polesworth
carrying with them the body of their Foundress.
This might have led Wendover to believe that
Eadgith lived at Polesworth : he is too exact in
the date of her death to have mistaken her in
any way for the much more ancient Edith who
was the sainted foundress of the house there.

Sorely must St. Edith and her community have
fared in the year 943, after Athelstan's death,
when Sihtric's son Anlaf marched to Tamworth,
which he "took by storm, and great slaughter
was made on either hand ; and the Danes had the
victory, and led away much booty. There during

the pillage was Wulfrun taken." Edmund the Elder gave up all the kingdom north of the Watling Street to his foe, and Tamworth thus passed into the hands of the Danes; but he soon got all back through a revolt of the Northumbrians and the death of Anlaf.

CHAPTER III.

EARLIER HISTORY OF THE COLLEGIATE CHURCH.

EDGAR the Peaceful sat on the English throne from the year 959 to 975. He founded the Church of Tamworth afresh and gave it a College of Canons. This is thought to have been about the year 963. Perhaps the Church was now established again after the direful sacking of the town by Anlaf. If the canonization of St. Edith took place (as it most likely did) in the reign of Edgar, the religious practices of his faith would lead him soon to set about a lasting monument to one whose ties of kindred even claimed some homage at his hand. Either now or later on after her death the Church was solemnly consecrated in honour of his beatified aunt. As the fame of the Saint spread abroad so the people from all the country around flocked more and more to Tamworth on her festival, which was kept with great solemnity for the seven following days making up the full festal *octave*. In time they brought in the merchandize of goods and cattle, and what was begun in worship went on with traffic too. A yearly fair thus sprung up, and the Church had the tolls which at last belonged to it by prescriptive right.

In Edgar's reign the Archbishop of Canterbury put *Regulars*, or monks, very generally throughout his province into the minsters and large churches, in place of the *Secular* or common Clergy. It seems as if at first the Regular Clergy were at Tamworth. Wulfric Spot, who founded the Abbey of Burton-on-Trent in the year 1002 and died in 1010, had an interest in this town by holding lands here. Now, in his will he left an estate at Longdon in Staffordshire to the Convent of Tamworth, who were to have half the fruit of it and the Monks of Burton the other half, in food, men, herds, and all things. The will runs thus : " & ic geann thon hirede in Tamwurdin th' lande æt Langandune ealswa hi hit me ær toleton. & habban hi thone bryce healfne. & healfne tha munecas into B. ge on mete. ge on mannon. ge on yrfe. ge on ælcon thingon." Which Dugdale gives in Latin : "Item do conventui in Tamwurthin fundum illum apud Langandune, sicut ipsi (monachi) illum mihi antehac locarunt, & habeant ipsi usum fructum (ejus) dimidium, & dimidium monachi Byrtonenses, cum in cibariis, tum in hominibus, tum in pecudibus, tum in rebus omnibus." But *convent* was often used for any community or body of men. Be this as it may, it is certain that after the Conquest the Dean and

Canons of Tamworth were secular, although in the year 1220 we find them once called monks.

In the host of warriors who came into England in the year 1066 when the hapless country fell into the thraldom of Duke William of Normandy, was Robert le Marmion lord of Fontenay near Caen. On the deadly battle-plain of Hastings he shewed great bravery, seeking out Harold to slay him as a foe forsworn to William. Robert Wace, whose father was in that fight, thus rhymes of of him in his *Roman de Rou.*

> " E li sire de Fontenei
> De Robercil e del Molei
> Vunt demandant Heraut li Rei
> As Engleiz dient: ça estez,
> U est li reis ke vos servez
> Ki a Guillame est parjurez?
> Morz est s'il pot estre trovez."

William paid back his followers for their services with vast estates wrested from the native owners of the soil. Robert le Marmion had lands given him in the counties of Warwick, Leicester, and Lincoln. There are reasons almost as strong as proofs for believing that he was the royal steward and as such is called in Domesday, Robert Dispensator. He had the Castle of Tamworth with its many knights-fees in Leicestershire and Warwickshire and the Manor of Scrivelsby with *its* fees in Lincolnshire, all which together formed one barony, as is seen in the records of the Royal Exchequer for the year 1304. And with the barony went the famous office of Royal Champion for defending by arms the title of the king to his throne when he was being crowned.

Camden and other later writers suppose that one of the first Norman lords of the Castle rebuilt the Church and made it collegiate. Certainly they did not place the College here, still the oldest parts of the present fabric of the Church are in the earliest Norman style, though not so old as the ruins of the Deanery. And that might have been the time for a change from Regular to Secular Canons, when the Church became attached to the Marmion barony. The College was formed of six Prebends. These were, Amington or the Deanery, Syerscote, Wilnecote, Coton, Bonehill, and Wigginton and Comberford: all townships or hamlets within the Parish of Tamworth, which seems to have now the same boundaries as it had in those olden times.

The Parish with the Liberty of the Castle contains 12,420 acres. The population in 1801 was 5337; and in 1861, 10,192. The names of the townships and hamlets within the Parish are thus given in some quaint, hobbling rhymes common amongst the country-folks here in the middle of the last century.

" There's Biterscote, and Bonehill, and Dunstall upon Dun,
Hopwas, and Coton, and miry Wiginton,
Little Amington, and Great Amington, with the Woodhouses by,
Glascote, and Wilnecote, and merry Fasely,
Comberford, and Syerscote, and Bole Hall Street,
And Tamworth is the Head Town where all these Cuckolds meet."

Kettlebrook, Two-Gates, and Aldermills had not then arisen to claim a share in this rugged chaunt.

For two hundred years after the Norman Conquest very little is found concerning the Church. Henry II. made some presentations to the Prebends; and this might have been done whilst the demesnes of the Castle were in the hands of the king between the death of Robert le Marmion fifth lord and the succession of his son Robert. In 1199 Simon a Canon of Tamworth carried a plea of land in the king's court from Easter (May 16th) into Trinity Octave against the Knight-Templars of Warwickshire. And about 1250, or at least between 1222 and 1253, Nicholas a Canon and W. a chaplain of Tamworth with Alexander chaplain of Cotes (Coton) and many others witnessed a charter of Ralph Basset confirming some of his ancestors' gifts to the Priory of Canwell. Henry III. presented Ralph de Hotote, Mar. 23rd 1266-7, to a Prebend here void by the death of Simon a royal chaplain.

In 1220 it was found that the Canons of Tamworth received in Leicestershire, at Burrow two parts of the tithes of corn of all the demesnes in the same parish *ab antiquo;* at Somerby two parts of the tithes of corn of the demesne of Will. Panton *ab antiquo* which the Nuns of Langley then held for 5*s.* : and the *Monks* of Tamworth received at Stony Stanton the tithes of corn of the ancient demesne of Will. Basset *de antiquo*. Various inquisitions show that in those places lands were held of the Castle of Tamworth at each by the service of one knights-fee.

By fine levied in the king's court at Easter 1257 the Dean and Chapter of Tamworth bought of Sir Philip Marmion the advowson of the Church of Middleton in Warwickshire. They gave 10*l.* sterling for it and were to pay yearly within the Abbey of Merevale ten marks (6*l.* 13*s.* 4*d.*) to Will. de Farnham, half at Michaelmas and half at Easter, but after his death they were to be free of this payment. And thus it was that for nearly three hundred years this Chapter always appointed a stipendary to serve at Middleton.

The Dean and Chapter of Tamworth were also lords of the manor of Middleton, but we cannot find how it came to them. Sir Philip Marmion and his descendants all held the manor, of this Church *in capite* by the yearly service of half a mark. Middleton as well as the Castle here was a country-seat of the Marmions. At both places Sir Philip passed his time when the turmoils of war and the duties of the royal court were over and pleasure led him to hunt, hawk, and fish in the neighbourhood of Tamworth. He often chased the deer in the royal forest of Cannock, and once he had to receive the king's pardon (Jan. 26th 1261-2) because his hounds in running some does there started and took a brocket. It seems likely too that he closed his life at Middleton, at least all his coheiresses were abiding there just after he died.

Sir Henry de Hastings forfeited his estates to the crown and amongst them the manor of Wigginton with the Staffordshire side of Tamworth in the year 1266, being one' of the leaders in the great outbreak of the barons against Henry III. wherein he made himself noted by fiercely holding out Kenilworth Castle when it was closely beset by the royal army. The king rewarded the faithful services of Sir Philip Marmion and bestowed on him for life the rebel's manor with both the Staffordshire and Warwickshire sides of the town. In the inquisition taken at Tamworth Sep. 11th in the same year for making the grant it was found that the Dean and Canons of the Church received the issues of the fairs here, but those of the markets pertained to the king and were valued a-year, with pleas, fines, and perquisites of courts, at 50s. on each side of the town. At that time the only fair was on the festival of St. Edith: two more fairs were established in the year 1336.

Pope Nicholas IV. in the year 1288 granted the tenths of all church-benefices to Edward I. for six years towards the expenses of a Crusade. In 1291 the taxation of the province of Canterbury was finished. The Church of St. Edith in the Deanery of Tamworth and Tutbury was then valued at (fifty-five marks) 36*l.* 13*s.* 4*d.*, the tenth being (five marks and a half) 3*l.* 13*s.* 4*d.* And the Church of Berkeswell in Warwickshire was valued at (twenty marks) 13*l.* 6*s.* 8*d.* over and above the pension of (one mark) 13*s.* 4*d.* which the Prebendal Church of Tamworth received in it, the tenth of the pension being 1*s.* 4*d.*

The Rural Deanery of Tamworth and Tutbury then took in the Churches of Hanbury, Tutbury, Rolleston, Burton-on-Trent, Tatenhill, Yoxhall, Ridware, Elford, Clifton, Shenstone, Alrewas, Walsall, Bromwich, Handsworth, Tamworth, and Wednesbury, in Staffordshire.

An inquisition made at Tamworth Mar. 13th 1291-2 gives nearly the same valuation as in the Taxation of Pope Nicholas. It is said that the Church was in the gift of Sir Philip Marmion when he died, and in it were six Prebends. Of these Prebends, John de Teford had the Deanery valued in common years at 10*l.*, Master Robert de Pygford one valued at 7*l.*, Ralph de Heneham one at 6*l.*, Hugh de Cave one valued in all issues at 5*l.*, Master Michael (de Ormesby) one valued in all issues at 4*l*, and Master Adam de Waltone one at 4*l.* Total value with the advowson 36*l.*

Sir Philip Marmion seventh Norman Lord of the Castle was the last baron of his family. He died in the autumn of 1291 leaving four coheiresses to succeed him. By his first wife Jane daughter and coheiress of Hugh de Kilpeck he had three daughters, Jane, Mazera, and Matilda; and by his second wife Mary (on whom and his issue by her he entailed Scrivelsby) he had another daughter Jane. The elder Jane born in 1255 had been married to William Morteyn, but

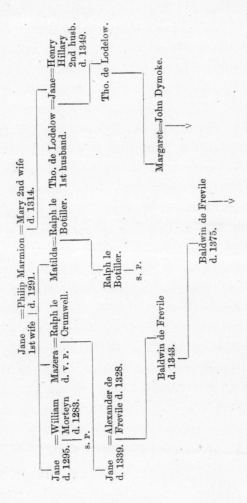

he was now dead; she became the eighth *Lady* of the Castle and died in 1295 without issue. Mazera was married to Ralph le Crumwell; she died in her father's life-time, leaving a daughter Jane born in 1267 who was now wife of Alexander de Frevile and to whom the Castle passed from her aunt. Matilda born in 1261 was married to Ralph le Botiller: her only son Ralph died childless leaving a cousin of the same name as his heir. The younger Jane born in 1283 was only eight years old when her father died, and became a ward of the crown: her first husband was Thomas de Lodelow by whom she had a son Thomas, whose daughter Margaret was wife of Sir John Dymoke ancestor of the Dymokes of Scrivelsby; her second husband was Henry Hillary. Lady Mary outlived her husband Sir Philip Marmion until 1314. Lady Jane de Frevile had a son Baldwin born in 1292 and deceased in 1343, and he too had a son Baldwin who was born in 1317 and died in 1375, one after the other Lords of the Castle.

Each of the coheiresses of Sir Philip Marmion took her share of the estates; but the right of presenting to the Church here fell to them turn by turn under agreements made amongst themselves. The advowson of the Prebends of Wilnecote and Coton was granted by the king in dowery to Lady Mary Marmion and she died seized of them, but had passed all her life-interest over to Sir Ralph Basset of Drayton. At Epiphany 1293-4 the king challenged the advowson of the Church to belong to the crown, on the plea that Henry II. was seized in his demesne as of fee and right etc. of presenting to the same Prebends William de Cap'lla his clerk etc. On the part of Lady Jane Morteyn and the others it was replied that Jane the youngest coheiress was under age and in the king's wardship and without her they could not answer. So the matter was to stand by till she came of age. And it was not brought on again.

Henry Hillary and Lady Jane his wife entered into the compositions with the rest of the coheiresses and their husbands, whereby whilst sole she presented her clerk to the Deanery, and Henry in her right his clerk to the Prebend of Wilnecote. These compositions were made without the king's licence. On that account after his wife's death Henry Hillary had to sue for a royal pardon. It was granted him Apr. 4th 1348 and at the same time leave was given for him and the heirs of Lady Jane to present according to the agreements. But Henry died Feb. 13th following. All the four coheiresses and their husbands were now dead. The dormant barony of Marmion rested in the Crown there to moulder for ever buried beneath the rubbish of ages deeper and deeper as generations swept along and overlaid it more and more with the off-shakings of countless families. Now too the advowson of the Prebends fell to the king and the Collegiate Church of Tamworth ranked among the Royal Free Chapels.

The Lord of the Castle did not easily yield to being stripped of the patronage of this Church and of other churches and chapels it seems in like manner. Sir Baldwin de Frevile kept up his claim for many years. As he was in the service of the Black Prince and much abroad in the wars against France he put Sir Fulk de Bermingham cavalier and John de Tamworth clerk in his place, in the year 1365, to prosecute in Chancery and other courts his *proparty* of the advowsons of the churches, prebends, and chapels falling to him by hereditary right after the deaths of Sir Philip Marmion, Lady Jane Morteyn, and Lady Jane de Frevile, and also of Sir Baldwin his father and others his ancestors. Sir Baldwin died Mar. 28th 1375. In the inquisition of his estates made soon after it was said that he held the advowson of the Deanery and five Prebends as pertaining to the Castle in fee-tail to himself and Ida his wife and their issue, and that the king had presented *one* Dean and several Prebendaries, but by what right the jurors did not know. It is true that by royal licence dated June 6th 1346 and by fine levied the next Michaelmas in the king's court Sir Baldwin had thus entailed the Castle and other estates, yet it was without anything being said as to the Church.

Nothing availed to unloose the iron-grasp which the Crown had fixed upon this Church.

CHAPTER IV.

LATER HISTORY OF THE COLLEGIATE CHURCH.

ON Trinity Monday (May 23rd) 1345 Tamworth was destroyed by fire. The Church too was burnt down. This sad mishap brought beggary on the larger part of the commonalty of the town. The inhabitants lost their houses, merchandise, goods, and chattels, and could not raise the usual taxes for the Crown. So they immediately petitioned the Parliament that for God and as a work of charity their fifteenths and tenths might be taken from the time of the fire according to the goods they had in hand and would hereafter have as God increased them, without regard to the amount paid before. At the intercession of Sir William de Clinton, Earl of Huntingdon (the bounteous founder of Maxtoke Priory) and other great men this reasonable petition was fully granted, and Aug. 28th following (three months after the fire) a royal mandate was issued for the collectors to take only the reduced taxes.

In 1349 a still greater affliction overtook Tamworth when the great pestilence on man and beast swept the whole kingdom and carried off a third of the population. The inhabitants of this town established for a time a *Sanatorium*, which might have been such a *Lazaretto* as the Italians were wont to set up outside their cities when the same fearful scourge was upon them.

Yet spite of the fire, and of the pestilence which vast floods foreran and famine followed, a noble Church was raised again. This was done no doubt with the aid of the country all around and of great and wealthy lords, who it was declared knew how much the town had suffered by the fire. In the windows and ancient pavement of the Church were once the arms of Clinton of Maxtoke, Clare, Bohun, Warren, Basset of Drayton, Basset of Blore, Frevile, Botetourt, Beauchamp of Warwick, Stafford of Clifton Campvile, and Comberford, also of the royal Plantagenets; all which high families may be supposed to have been benefactors at this time. But it was many a year before the building was finished. There were four *Wardens of the Work of the Church* to receive the alms and to overlook the fabric and the workmen. These Wardens were Richard le Whelere, John de Cosseby, John le Newman, and Nicholas le Blound, some of the foremost inhabitants of the town. To them and to the Wardens after them Milisand once wife of Adam atte

Castel of Tamworth corveser by her deed dated
Jan. 22nd 1351-2 gave a plot of land with
buildings on it next *le Schirchstile* between the
Churchyard and the kings-way. They were to
let the land at as much as they could for the
work of the Church and above all "al ov'ayne de
n're Dame en lesgle,"—for the work of our Lady
within the Church.

Many changes afterwards made the Church a
very fine pile of buildings. Yet the endowment
of the establishment was exceedingly scanty and
barely gave a fitting support to the Clergy. The
Dean and Canons sometimes dwelt at Tamworth
where there was a Dean's House; but generally
the Prebends yielded only titles with trifling
incomes to clerks and others who seldom saw
the town. Each of the non-resident Canons had
his substitute or Vicar here in some poor clerk
who undertook the duties of his Prebend and his
charge in the Parish. These Vicars rarely come
into notice. In the court of Tamworth on the
Staffordshire side May 23rd 1429 this order
was made: "It' ordinatu' est q'd nemo habiat
nullu' vicariu' ec'e ad tabila' sua' sub pena vj^s· &
viij^d·." A royal precept dated Nov. 7th 1458
charged the bailiffs of the same side that as
ecclesiastics were not bound to the views of
frank-pledge unless for some special cause they
should not distrain upon Will. Bolter, David
Byffeld, Rich. Sturgeys, Tho. Aleyn, Tho. Hull,

and Rich. Tatenell, Vicars of the King's Chapel of Tamworth, to appear at those courts; and if any distresses had been already taken in the matter they were to be restored. As a body the Vicars were amerced in small sums for not doing suit at some of the leets between the years 1499 and 1517.

A few curious bye-laws appear on the rolls of the great courts of the Staffordshire side of the town. Oct. 13th 1388: if any man has money belonging to the Church he shall pay half at Martintide and half at Christmas, under pain of entry upon his lands etc. Nov. 14th 1390: no man, woman, or servant to go out after the curfew from one place to another unless they have a light in their hands, under pain of imprisonment. Oct. 15th 1448: the Dean of the Church to ring a bell at 3 o'clock in the morning. Many orders were made respecting the Churchyard.

It was the duty of the Dean and Canons or their Vicars to celebrate Mass with all solemnities and to say the Canonical Hours publicly every day. But in the earlier part of Henry VI.'s reign through poverty divine service had sunk to the lowest ebb, standing in well-known need of help, and more so when the Vicars Choral appointed for the services and for the cure of souls and mostly attached to the Prebendal Chapels had to be administering the Sacraments out of the Church particularly at the great fes-

4

tivals. As the Vicars were very few and were thus away the Canonical Hours had ceased and the solemnities in Mass had been laid aside; and thus divine worship was so much curtailed as to bring scandal on the Church and harm to the faithful. Such had been the state of things for some time when the Dean John Bate finding that any amendment could hardly be looked for except through the aid of some bountiful person petitioned Henry VI. for relief.

The king felt all the more called upon to protect this Church as it was in the royal patronage and the foundation of his illustrious progenitors. So he furnished means for placing two more chaplains here. By letters patent dated Feb. 9th 1445-6 a perpetual chantry was established in the Church, to which the Dean was to appoint a chaplain who should take an oath of residence here and of obedience to him. This chaplain was to celebrate Mass daily at the altar of the Holy Trinity for the peace of England and France, for the good estate of the king and his consort Margaret living or dead, and for the souls of the king's father and mother, of his forefathers, and of all the faithful. He was also to serve in the Canonical Hours, High Masses, and other daily divine offices, as the Dean ordered. For his support he was to have the fee-farm rent of 116s. hitherto yielded to the Crown for the Warwickshire side of the town to be paid him directly by the bailiffs four times a-year in equal portions; and he might freely receive an endowment of lands and rents to the value of 100*s*. notwithstanding the mortmain or any other statute. Moreover royal license was given to the Dean to found another perpetual chantry at the altar of the Blessed Virgin and in honour of the holy virgins Edith and Katherine. To it also he was to appoint a chaplain to celebrate Mass daily for the two kingdoms, for the king and queen, and for the Dean himself, for the souls of Robert and Alice his father and mother, their parents and benefactors, and of all the departed. This chaplain too was to serve in the other daily Masses and services; and for his maintenance the foundation might be freely endowed by the Dean with lands and rents worth twelve marks (8*l*.) a-year. And farther the king granted to the Vicars Choral and chaplains a tun of red wine every year out of the royal wines in the port of Bristol, for the Masses, so that the people might oftener and more diligently draw nigh unto the venerable Sacrament of the Body and Blood of Christ.

In the broken series of Henry VI.'s Royal Household accounts it is seen that the Vicars of Tamworth had their wine for the years 1447 and 1448. But the *Chantry of King Henry VI.* and the *Chantry of Dean Bate* had scarcely been set on foot when the Parliament in the year 1450 recruiting the Royal Exchequer passed a sweeping

Act of Resumption to make void the king's gifts from the beginning of his reign. And thus the grant to this Church came to nothing.

Still the Church went forward for the better. Henry Jekes a native of the town and one of the High Bailiffs for the Staffordshire side elected in the year 1470 gave a house and garden to the Vicars Choral for their continual residence and "entercomyng together." This became the *Mansion-house for the Priests of the College* or *College House*. In the making of the gift the royal licence of Henry VI. had been secured in which the Vicars were formed into a body corporate so as to have the house in succession for ever. This incorporation and a standing composition that the Vicars were to be perpetual and not removeable (save when the Dean and Canons whose places they held came to reside) gave to the working staff of clergy a stability it never had before. Many gifts and foundations of obits followed which we here notice : only the first gift was before the incorporation.

At the Staffordshire court of Tamworth Aug. 30th 1445 Nicholas Pydde gave two burgages in *Lichefeldestret* to John, Archbishop of Canterbury ; John Bate, Dean ; Rob. Monter, Will. Pydde, John Lynton, Will. Rous, Tho. Asshecombe, and John Longedon, clerks, and their heirs for ever.

There was a Chantry of St. George the Martyr

within this Church, and the chaplain was bound not only "to sing morowe masse dayly in Seynt Georgs Chappell there" but also to teach a Free School in the Parish. Many persons gave lands and tenements for finding a priest continually in this twofold charge. A Guild of St. George too flourished throughout the town : this Brotherhood had land worth 5*l.* a-year, and that income at last being given for the purpose with other rents from a benefactor a Grammar School was erected. John Bailey was open-handed towards his native town in the way of education. By his will he founded a fellowship in St. John's College, Cambridge, and gave the first choice in it to the Parish of Tamworth; and he sought to make the Free School more enduring by placing the Chantry under the safety of a royal licence which it did not enjoy before. He therefore desired to establish the perpetual Chantry long ago set up here. It was to be of one chaplain who was to celebrate Mass every Lord's day for the good estate of Henry VIII. and Queen Jane living and dead, and for the souls of Henry VII. and Elizabeth his consort, of John Bailey himself and Agnes his wife, and of all the faithful departed. And moreover the chaplain was to keep a Free School of Grammar at Tamworth and teach all *honest* persons, without salary, stipend, reward, or gift. Bailey's executors (Nicholas Agard gent. and John Shephard chaplain) had the royal grant July 16th 1536 for this *Chantry of John Bailey* and mortmain-licence to endow it with lands and rents to the clear yearly value of 6*l.* Thus they increased the living for the St. George Priest by buying more lands and making them over to him. Leland says, "There is a Guild of St. *George* in *Tamworth,* and to it belonged 5.*l.* Land *per an.* and of late one Johne Bailie gave other 5.*l.* Land unto it, and therewith is now erected a Grammar-Schoole."

In the year 1548 St. George's Chantry was held by Richard Broke or Brooke clerk. According to the official Certificates of Chantries the yearly value of it was 12*l.* 18*s.* 3½*d.* which reprises (35*s.* 3¼*d.*) brought down to 11*l.* 3*s.* 0¼*d.*; but the chaplain's clear portion was 10*l.* 13*s.* 2¼*d.* or according to other accounts ¼*d.* more. There also belonged to it 6 oz. of plate parcel-gilt, ornaments worth 2*s.* 10*d.*, and a "vessel vsed to be letten out for rep'açons of the t'ents belonging to the possessyons therof"—given in security for loans of money and afterwards redeemed—32*s.* 2*d.*

Richard Bretton or Breton (who died we find about 1518) gave some land to have a Mass every Friday in the Church and an obit once a year. The yearly value in 1548 was 29*s.* 4*d.*, out of which 26*s.* 6*d.* (included above) had been always given to the Morrow Mass Priest and Schoolmaster leaving 2*s.* 10*d.* for the obit, with no reprises: no plate nor goods.

At this time too the endowment is again thus set forth in the Ministers' Accounts and in the later grants of the Crown.

A messuage and land in Bolehall held by Tho. Aynsworth for 21*s.* a year; a croft of land or moor in Dosthill in Kingsbury Parish, by John Aynsworth for 3*s.*; piece of arable land in Wilnecote, by John Colman for 16*d.*; piece of arable land there, by Will. Michell for 10*d.*; a messuage and garden on the Warwickshire side and croft on the Staffordshire side of the town, by Edw. Mylner for 7*s.*; five messuages and gardens on the Warwickshire side of the town, severally by Will. Edes or Ees for 2*s.*, John Hewer for 14*s.*, John Blodeworth for 8*s.*, John Chare for 10*s.*, and John Clark for 5*s.*; seven messuages and gardens on the Staffordshire side of the town held severally by John Sponer for 6*s.* 8*d.*, Hen. Seale for 11*s.*, Rob. Bucknell for 5*s.* 4*d.*, John Carpenter for 6*s.*, Will. Rogers for 5*s.*, Will. Harrison for 12*s.*, and Humfr. Torre for 7*s.*; also the messuage and garden called *the Mansion House of the Priest* or *Scole house* by Richard Broke clerk for 10*s.*: total 6*l.* 15*s.* 2*d.* But there were some reprises: to Sir Edw. Aston knt. and Rich. Leveson lords of Bolehall 18*d.*, to the Bailiffs of the Staffordshire side of the town 4*s.* 9*d.*, to those of the Warwickshire side 19*d.*, and to Jane Robinson *lady* of Drayton Basset 10*s.* 2*d.*: total 18*s.* Clear yearly value 5*l.* 17*s.* 2*d.*

To this endowment the executors of John
Bailey had added the following. Some pieces of
land held by Will. Batkyns for 25s. a-year;
parcels of meadow and pasture in Coton, by
Henry Alred for 40s.; pieces of land, by Will.
Buckley for 9s. 1d.; parcels of land, by the same
for 16s. 6½d.; a croft of land and close of meadow
and parcels of land and pasture in Wilnecote,
severally by Rog. Wright for 9s., Agnes Botte for
4s., Tho. Bek for 9s., and Will. Coton for 2s. 4d.;
and two closes of pasture in Dosthill, severally
by Rob. Melbourne for 7s., and Rich. Cowper for
4s.: total 6l. 5s. 11½d. Reprises: to Humfrey
Comberford, Esq., lord of Wigginton for Alred's
tenement 3s. 0¾d.; to the same for Buckley's
tenement 3s. 2½d.; to the lord of the Manor of
Comberford for Buckley's other tenement 13d.;
and to Jane Robinson widow for the tenement
in Dosthill 3s. 9d.: total 11s. 1¼d. Clear yearly
value 5l. 14s. 10¼d.

This second statement which estimates the endowment at 13l. 1s. 1½d. reprises at 1l. 9s. 1¼d.
and the clear yearly value at 11l. 12s. 0¼d. seems
to be correct. In the first there was probably no
rent-charge on the School House.

The history of the Chantry of St. George is the
early history of the present Free Grammar School.

There were also endowments for two chaplains
in this Church. Thomas Barwell and Thomas
Grent separately gave rent and land for main-

taining the Lady Chapel within the Church and another Chapel in the Churchyard; and they desired to be perpetually prayed for. Barwell's gift consisted of a yearly rent of 4s. paid by the Chapelwardens of Wilnecote out of land there let in 1548 to John Lewes; Grent's gift was a garden in Tamworth and two butts of land in Millfield let to Lawrence Damport for 8d. and 4d. Total yearly value 5s.; no reprises: no plate nor goods.

Sir Thomas Ferrers knt. Lord of the Castle Feb. 10th 1495 [1495-6] for the health of his soul and the souls of Anne his wife, of John his son and heir, and of their forefathers, gave to the perpetual Vicars here a yearly rent of 26s. 8d. out of the water-mill called *Astforde Myll*, two pastures etc. at Claverley in Shropshire which he lately had of Hen. Colle. The Vicars were to celebrate three weekly Masses of Requiem, and on the yearly festival of Saint   being the day of Sir Thomas's death Mass and obsequies for the souls abovenamed.

The following perpetual foundations for yearly obits except the last one were made by chief inhabitants of the town, who often held some public office in the reigns of Henry VII. and Henry VIII. The names of the tenants of the lands and yearly values are set down here as they stood in 1548.

Humfrey Jacob gave 1a. of meadow in *Broode*

Medowe and 3*a.* of land in Wigginton for an obit. Let to Edw. Broks for 4*s.* 8*d.*

Richard Dalton gave 1*a.* of meadow in *Calforde Medowe* for an obit.

Thomas Meire gave another acre in the same *Caldeforde Meadow* for an obit. Let with the last to Rog. Bukland for 6*s.* 8*d.*; reprise 15*d.* to lord of Wigginton, leaving 5*s.* 5*d.*

Thomas Tayler gave a shop in the *Market place* for an obit. Let to Edw. Ascall for 3*s.* 4*d.*; reprise 1*d.* to the bailiffs of the Warwickshire side, leaving 3*s.* 3*d.*

Richard Baxter gave a croft in Drayton Basset for an obit. Let to Rob. Wilkox for 10*s.*; reprise 12*d.* to the capital lord of Drayton Basset, leaving 9*s.*

Henry Cowper gave a messuage in Wilnecote for an obit. Let to Tho. Carter for 8*s.*; reprise 7*d.* to the capital lord of Wilnecote, leaving 7*s.* 5*d.*

William Paynell gave two butts of arable land in Tamworth Fields on the Warwickshire side for an obit. Let to Tho. Carter for 9*d.*

John Geffrey gave a croft and parcel of land in Amington for an obit. Let to Rog. Payne for 8*s.* 6*d.*; reprise 22*d.* to the capital lord of Amington for 1 ℔ of pepper, leaving 6*s.* 8*d.*

John Seale gave a messuage and parcels of land in Amington for an obit. Let to Will. Seale for 3*s.* 4*d.*

John Price clerk gave a garden in *Bowbrige-strete* and Leonard Ferrers gent (son of Sir Thomas Ferrers) a messuage and garden there for an obit each. All let to John Broughton for 8*s.*; reprise 12*d.* to the Warwickshire bailiffs, leaving 7*s.*

Thomas Wright gave a messuage and garden in *Colehill* for an obit. Let to Alice Shamond for 5*s.*

The same Thomas Wright gave 1*r.* of meadow and seven butts or selions of arable land in Wigginton for another obit. Let to Rog. Bukland for 18*d.*

John Irpe gave a messuage and garden in *Gungate* Warwickshire side for an obit. Let to John Bot for 7*s.*; reprise 8*d.* to the Warwickshire bailiffs, leaving 6*s.* 4*d.*

Richard Freman clerk gave a messuage and garden in *Gungate* adjoining the last for an obit. Let to John Wright for 9*s.*; reprise 16*d.* to the Warwickshire bailiffs, leaving 7*s.* 8*d.*

John Mathewe gave a messuage and garden in *Church Strete* Warwickshire side for an obit. Let to John Harison for 5*s.*

Tho. Baker *alias* Dixson gave a messuage and garden in *Churchestrete* for an obit. Let to Rich. Seale for 4*s.*

Peter Goabowt gave *Dovehowse Croft* on the Staffordshire side of the town for an obit. Let to Edw. Broks for 3*s.* 4*d.*; reprise 6*d.* to the Staffordshire bailiffs, leaving 2*s.* 10*d.*

William Wilkoks and William Irpe gave a messuage in *Bulstokewelstrete* [east end of George St.] for an obit each. Let to Ralph Shosmyth for 6s. 8d.

John Abell and John Coton gave a messuage at *Cockett lane ende* near the Church bringing in 4s. a-year for an obit.

William Akeyley gave a messuage and garden in *Lichfeldstrete* for an obit. Let to Roger Bukland for 9s. 4d.; reprises to the lord of Drayton Basset (Jane Robinson) 2s. and to the bailiffs of Tamworth 4d., leaving 7s.

John à Grene gave a messuage and small garden in *Lichfeldstrete* for an obit. Let to Will. Hartell for 6s. 8d.; reprise 6½d. to the Staffordshire bailiffs, leaving 6s. 1½d.

The total sum of these obits was 7l. 1s. 5d. reprises 11s. 1½d. leaving clear 6l. 10s. 3½d.

Lady Dorothy Ferrers widow of Sir John Ferrers knt. bought for 18l. Sept. 18th 1526 lands, meadows, and pastures of the clear yearly value of 25s. which Ralph Lago of Tamworth yeoman had in the fee of Wigginton. And in July 1528 she bought of Richard Bowers of Northampton clothier and Margery his wife a burgage for which he had given twenty marks two years before. The burgage "in the strete called le Buchere" betwixt the burgage of Humfrey Ferrers, Esq. and that of John Jekes stretched from the kings-way to the ground

of the Vicars of the College. The east end of
Church Street was then Butcher Street or the
Butchery, and the Mansion-house or College of
the Vicars stood in Cokets Lane (now College
Lane) on the site of the present National Schools.
By deed Oct. 20th 1530 Lady Dorothy passed
the lands and burgage in trust to eight persons
and their sons and heirs-apparent : Will. Repington of Little Amington gent. and Francis his
son, John Jekes of Tamworth gent. and Richard
his son, John Wodshawe of Tamworth chapman
and John his son, Tho. Golson of Tamworth and
Humf. his son, Rich. Coton of Coton yeoman and
John his son, Nich. Golson of Drayton Basset yeo.
and John his son, John Darlaston of Wigginton
yeo. and John his son, and Nich. Melbourne of
Wigginton yeo. and John his son; their heirs and
assigns. She then declared the uses of the trust.
The bailiffs were to receive the issues. Every
year on July 11th they were to have an obit in
the Church with the whole choir, and a solemn
Dirge sung on the evening of the same day and
Mass of Requiem on the next morning, then
specially to pray for the souls of Sir John Ferrers
her late husband, of Dame Dorothy herself, of
William Harper, Esq. and Margaret his wife her
father and mother, and of all Christians. Each
of the Vicars being at the Dirge and saying Mass
on the morrow for these souls to have 6*d.* for
his labour. To each of the two Deacons 3*d.* For

ringing the two knells 8*d.* For the hire of four tapers to burn about the herse in the time of the service 8*d.* To the bellman [for crying the services throughout the town] 2*d.* To poor people of the town at their houses at the discretion of the bailiffs 6*s.* 8*d.* Each of the four bailiffs to offer a half-penny at the Requiem and to take 4*d.* for his labour. And the Vicars to have 8*d.* a-year to pray for the souls in their bead-roll. The Grey Friars at Lichfield were also at the same time to sing Dirge by note and Mass of Requiem : also the [Augustinean] Friars of Atherstone. And if three or four soul-priests were serving in Tamworth Church during the obit each of them was to have 4*d.* so that he said the Dirge and Requiem. What was over of the rents was to be locked up in a box and used to repair the premises. The bailiffs were to have the key and the box was to be delivered to the St. George Priest.

Lady Dorothy Ferrers fell ill and July 24th 1532 made her will. She desired to be buried within this Church by the side of her husband, and bequeathed, to the high altar 10*s.*, to maintain the canopy and to the body of the Church 20*s.*, and 10*l.* to bring her *whome* and for her month's mind. The obit was to be kept as she had ordained by indenture in three parts, of which one was to be kept with the Dean's deputy [Vicar] in the treasure-house, another with William Repington and his heirs, and the third with the St. George Priest so that the bailiffs might resort to it and know what to do. And she bequeathed to the high altar her black damask gown for a vestment with her arms upon it; and her executors were to make it of her own goods. Very soon after Lady Dorothy was carried *home* indeed, and laid to rest with her husband beneath the marble altar-tomb which had been put up to their joint memories.

Several other endowments existed about 1540 for particular foundations; but our researches have failed to bring their history fully to light. A barn and croft on the Staffordshire side were for the perpetual maintenance of a priest to celebrate Mass of *Our Lady of Grace*. Two cottages in *Lichfeldstrete* (perhaps Pydde's gift in 1445) were for an obit. Some crofts of land and pasture called *Pristley Feeldes* and *Pristley Riddings* on the Staffordshire and Warwickshire sides were for a chaplain to celebrate *the firste Masse* in the Church. *Martin's Crofte* on the Warwickshire side belonged to the College. Part of these may have been included in our former accounts. Moreover there were lands, meadows, and pastures on both sides of the town for the maintenance of a priest celebrating here, and for obits, lamps, lights, and such uses, and ten acres of land were occupied by the Churchwardens and others for the like manifold purposes.

There were four chapels within the Parish. Those at Amington and Wilnecote were older than the time of Edward III., for in the year 1341 they were taxed in the ninth of corn, wool, and lambs to the king. Amington was thus valued at ten marks, the ninth at 6 marks 5s. 8d., and the glebe with the tithes of hay etc. was worth 47s. 8d. a-year. Wilnecote was taxed at six marks, the ninth at four marks, and the glebe with the tithes was worth two marks a-year.

Wilnecote Chapel was for the ease of the inhabitants "being two myles distaunt from their p'yshe churche, and fowle ways betwene." It was endowed with land worth 36s. a-year and no reprises in 1548, and then possessed neither plate nor goods. Wigginton Chapel was founded later and had land given to it "for hiring of a priest to syng in the seid chappell at suche tyme as for fowlenes of the Wether thenh'itants there cannot convenyently go to their p'ishe churche of Tamworth :" in 1548 this land was valued at 2s. 8d. a-year; no reprises: no plate nor goods. Fazeley Free Chapel standing in the time of Henry VII. was endowed with Fazeley Mill and had a cottage of one chamber for the priest.

Many aids or subsidies were wrung from the clergy by Henry VIII. to fill again his oft-drained coffers. In 1533 the Church of Tamworth was taxed in the following manner. Mr. Tho. Perker, Dean, 32s. Mr. John Fyssher, Prebendary of

Syerscote, 3s. 1¼d. Mr. Will. Westcote, Prebendary of Wilnecote, 8s. 10½d. Mr. Tho. Hall, Prebendary of Coton, 9s. 4d. Mr. John Wylcocks, Prebendary of Bonehill, 9s. 4d. Mr. Rog. Dyngley, Prebendary of Wigginton, 10s. Vicars Choral and Stipendaries; Mr. Geo. Planckeney, Mr. John Bee, Mr. John Lysett, Mr. Will. Crokell, Mr. Geoffrey Hatheryngton, Mr. Tho. Scheymon, Mr. Tho. Pyrre, Mr. Rog. de Wylmecote, and Mr. John Brette, 5s. 4d. each; Mr. John Walker, Mr. Ralph Mere, Mr. Ralph Wilcocks, 4s. 5¼d. each.

In the year 1534 Henry VIII. took to himself the title and office of Supreme Head on earth of the English and Irish Church. The Church of England departed from communion with the See of Rome, and the king ruled in doctrine and discipline as well as in its temporal possessions. The next year Parliament annexed to the Crown the first-fruits of benefices and spiritual dignities and the tenth of the yearly incomes of all livings. Thereon a valuation was taken by royal command in these matters. The account of the Spiritualities and Temporalities of the College of Tamworth in 1535 was thus given by the Commissioners of enquiry for Staffordshire who were Sir John Talbot and Sir John Gyfford knts.; Walt. Wrottesley, Esq., and John Grosvenour gent.

The Dean and Canons had together in common, lands and tenements called the glebe of the Pre-

6

bends to the yearly value of 4*l.* 7*s.* 8*d.*, of which each had his part. Master Thomas Parker, Dean, had of this glebe 13*s.* 4*d.*; and of tithes, oblations, and other spiritual emoluments, 20*l.* 6*s.* 8*d.* : total 21*l.* a-year, the tenth being 42*s.* Master John Fysher, Prebendary of Syerscote, had of the glebe 24*s.* 3*d.* ; and of tithes, oblations, and other spiritual emoluments 42*s.* 5*d.* : total 3*l.* 6*s.* 8*d.* a-year, the tenth being 6*s.* 8*d.* Master Rich. Pygot, Prebendary of Wilnecote, had of the glebe 13*s.* 11*d.* ; and of tithes, oblations, and other spiritual emoluments 7*l.* 6*s.* 1*d.* : total 8*l.*, the tenth being 16*s.* Master Tho. Hall, Prebendary of Coton, had of the glebe 8*s.* 3*d.* ; of a yearly pension paid by Master Rog. Dyngley, Prebendary of Wigginton, 40*s.* ; and of tithes, oblations, and other emoluments 5*l.* 11*s.* 9*d.*; total 8*l.*, the tenth being 16s. Master John Wylkoks, Prebendary of Bonehill, had in the glebe 17*s.* 8*d.* ; and of tithes and other spiritual emoluments 6*l.* 2*s.* 4*d.* : total 7*l.*, the tenth being 14*s.* Master Rog. Dyngley, Prebendary of Wigginton, had in the glebe 10*s.* 3*d.* ; and of tithes, oblations, and other spiritual emoluments, over and above the 40*s.* to Coton 9*l.* 9*s.* 9*d.* : total 10*l.*, the tenth being 20*s.*

John Leland visited Tamworth about the year 1541 and made some short but not faultless notes on the Church. "I sawe," says he, "but 3. notable Thinges in the Towne; the Paroch Church, the Castle, and the Bridge. The Collegiate Church

havinge a Deane and 6. Prebendaries, and every
one of these hath his Substitute there; but I
could not learne of whose Erection the Colledge
was. Some thinke it was a Colledge befor the
Conquest, others that it was of the Foundation of
Marmion, and that Opinion is most likely to be
true. *Marmions* without doubt were the successe
Lordes of the Castle. The King at this present is
taken as Patron of the Colledge. There be divers
fayre Tombes of Noblemen and Women in the
East Part of the Church, of th[e] *Freviles*, of
Baldwinus de Frevile L. of the Castle. There
lyeth alsoe the Grand-Father and Grand-Mother,
and Father and Mother of *Ferrers* nowe Owner
of *Tamworth* Castle."

But what this great Antiquary could not learn
was brought to light again when the Commissioners of Henry VIII. and those of Edward VI.
inquired into the foundations and revenues of
ecclesiastical establishments. A commission for
doing this was directed Feb. 9th, 1545-6, to
Richard bishop of Coventry and Lichfield; Sir
Philip Draycot knt.; Edw. Littleton, Esq.;
Anthony Bourchier gent.; and Will. Sheldon
gent.; or to three of them. They reported "the
college of Tomworth founded by Kynge Edgare
to fynd syx p'bendaryes to syng diuine s'vice wthin
the Collegiat & p'yshe Church of Tomworth."
The yearly revenues were thus employed. The
salaries of the Prebendaries according to their

several rates 55*l*. 17*s*. 9¾*d*.   The tenths 114*s*. 8*d*.
The wages of six priests to each of them 6*l*. paid
equally out of every Prebend, in all 36*l*.   The
Bishop's visitation 22*s*. 2¼*d*. Proxies and *Synags*
to the Archdeacon 18*s*. 4*d*.   A custom called *a
cheff ale* 33*s*. 4*d*.   The Deacon's wages 60*s*.   A
pension paid to the Prebend of Coton out of the
Prebend of Wigginton 43*s*. 4*d*.   Total 106*l*.9*s*.8*d*.,
the possessions not being charged with any ordi-
nary *resolutions* or deductions going out of them.
Fourscore and eight ounces of white plate; and
other goods and ornaments.   This Parish Church
had the cure of 2400 *howslyng people* (communi-
cants) in the Parish.

The gross yearly value of the revenues of the
Church is set forth in the leases of the Prebendal
temporalities from time to time to various parties.
The following were the last grants of that kind
made by the Dean and Canons of Tamworth.
Amington or the Deanery let to Tho. Jackson
Mar. 25th 1542 from three years to three years
for twenty-one years 27*l*. 7*s*.; Syerscote to Hugh
Lycet Mar. 18th 1546-7 for three years from the
next Lady-day 10*l*. 6*s*. 11*d*.; Wilnecote to Hen.
Colman Nov. 27th 1546 for three years from
the next Christmas 14*l*. 6*s*. 8*d*.; Coton to ......
Stamford 14*l*. 3*s*. 1*d*.; Wigginton to Rob. Har-
courte and John Horton Mar. 26th 1546 from
the 28th following for five years and so on for
twenty-one years 19*l*. 10*s*.; Bonehill to Hugh

Lee May 4th 1544 for sixty years from the next Ladyday 12*l*. 13*s*. 4*d*. Also the Rectory of Middleton in the tenure of John Willoughby 8*l*. Total yearly rents 106*l*. 7*s*.

CHAPTER V.

DISSOLUTION OF THE COLLEGE.

THE College of the Church was now close upon its end. In 1545 an Act of Parliament decreed the dissolution of such foundations, when the enquiry was made which we have mentioned. But Henry VIII. died before he reaped that golden harvest. Under Edward VI. another Act was passed Nov. 4th 1547 vesting Colleges, Chantries, and Free Chapels in the Crown. Sir John Talbott and Sir Geo. Blount knts., Reynold Corbett, Rich. Forssett and Rich. Cupper gents. were appointed Commissioners Feb. 14th and searched into what this Church possessed. Their certificate was returned into the Exchequer May 30th 1548. "The Colledge or churche Collegiate of Tamworth" they said was "Founded by kyng Edgare within the p'ishe churche of Tamworth, of one Deane, fyve p'bendaries and one lay Vicar Chorall p'petually to maynteyn dayly s'uice in the same churche; whiche Deane and p'bendaries ben p'son of the hol p'ishe of Tamworth." Yearly

value with the Mansion-house and garden of
the Vicars 102*l*. 9*s*. 11½*d*. Reprises in proxies
to the Bishop and synodals to the Archdeacon
40*s*. 7*d*. Remaining 100*l*. 9*s*. 4½*d*. Plate parcel-
gilt 10 oz. White plate 78¾ oz. Ornaments
12*l*. 7*s*. 6*d*. Implements in the Vicars' Mansion-
house 18*s*. 1*d*. Their account of the Chantry of
St. George, obits etc. has been already embodied
in our narrative. The Commissioners carried off
the plate, ornaments, and jewels; but they restored what was enough for the newly established
liturgy and services.

Elsewhere we find that the proxies to the
Bishop came to 67*s*. 6*d*. every three years; and
synodals to the Archdeacon to 18*s*. 1*d*. a-year:
total 40*s*. 7*d*. a-year just as the Commissioners
said.

But the Commissioners in their report missed
out much property belonging to the Church.
One of the sons of Lady Dorothy Ferrers was
tenant of what she had given for her obit, and
also of lands dedicated to the support of a priest
celebrating here and of some obits, lamps, and
lights; all which he kept close in his own hands.
Nor was he the only one who acted thus. The
Churchwardens and some parishioners or inhabitants of the town likewise held back lands
amounting to ten acres given for obits, lamps,
lights, and the support of a priest to celebrate;
and perhaps too, in part at least, those endowments

of which we have said we could not find the full
history, particularly the barn and croft for the
Mass of our Lady of Grace, Pristley Fields and
Pristley Riddings, and Martin's Croft. Such
great concealments almost seem to show either
that there was a plot in the town to withhold
information, or else that the Commissioners took
the part of silence in them. The lands were not
discovered till Elizabeth was on the throne, and
then they were seized by the Crown.

At the same time with the last commission an
enquiry was on hand as to the incomes of the
Dean, Canons, and Vicars, so that they might
have life-pensions given them in place of the
benefices whence they were ousted. Rich. Forssett
made his declaration June 30th which does not
quite tally with what the Commissioners had declared. He said that there were 1500 houselling
people; and that the clear yearly value of the
Church was 104*l*. 3*s*. 11*d*. The names and clear
yearly portions of the Prebendaries and Vicars
were as follows; and we add to each his allotted
pension. Simon Symons clerk, Dean, 18*l*. 18*s*. :
pension 6*l*. 13*s*. 4*d*. Rich. Pygott layman, Prebendary of Wilnecote, 7*l*. 4*s*. : pension 6*l*. Rob.
Johnson clerk, Prebendary of Bonehill, 4*l*.19*s*.4*d*.:
pension 4*l*. 19*s*. 4*d*. John Fyssher clerk, Prebendary of Syerscote, 64*s*. : pension 64*s*. Humf.
Horton clerk, Prebendary of Wigginton, 13*l*. 16*s*.
8*d*. : pension 6*l*. 13*s*. 4*d*. John Synger clerk,

Prebendary of Coton, 6*l*. 18*s*. 11½*d*. : pension 6*l*. John Pyndar, Deacon or lay Vicar Choral perpetual 60*s*. : pension 60*s*. Geffrey Hatherington clerk, Vicar for the Dean; Will. Crokehill, Vicar for the Prebendary of Wilnecote; Nich. Bageley or Baddesley, Vicar for the Prebendary of Bonehill, and Tho. Lesatt or Lesset, Vicar for the Prebendary of Syerscote, each 113*s*. 4*d*. : pension 100*s*. each. These last four Vicars prayed to be pensioned because they were perpetual and not removeable, according to the old composition; and their petition was granted.

A royal commission was issued June 20th 1548 to Sir Walter Mildmay knt. and Robert Keyleway, Esq., to settle what was to be done here for the maintenance of education and for the support and continuance of the new divine service and administration of Sacraments. These Commissioners visited Tamworth, and July 20th made their ordinations. They decreed, That the Grammar School should be continued, and Richard Broke was to remain Schoolmaster with the old stipend of 10*l*. 13*s*. 2½*d*. to be paid quarterly by the Receiver of the Court of Augmentations for Staffordshire: That the Church should remain undiminished as the Parish Church, and should have a Preacher of the divine word and two other Ministers to serve the cure, who should have for their habitation the house which the late Vicars of the College had enjoyed with the garden belonging; and the Preacher was to have 20*l*. and the Ministers or Curates 8*l*. a-year each paid quarterly for their maintenance.

These orders were carried out in the main, and the salaries were paid in the reigns of Edward VI., Mary, and Elizabeth, by the Crown Receivers for the counties of Stafford and Warwick. It was very easy to adapt the church-buildings to the new worship. The images were destroyed, the altars were taken down; and most likely the Canons' stalls were removed, as a Communion Table was placed in the middle of the Chancel. The Commissioners had given back for divine service,

> "Fyrste ij Challeses of Sylu' p'cell gylte w^t ij patents.
>
> ij Corporas w^t ther cases.
>
> one vestement of Red velvet w^t an albe.
>
> one vestement of blacke damaske.
>
> one vestement of grene satten of Burgis w^t an albe.
>
> one cope.
>
> iij alter clothes & iij towells.
>
> ij brason Candelstykes."

These served for the first Liturgy of Edward VI. compiled in 1548 but not made binding till the following year. Then the second Book of Common Prayer was put forth in 1552, and farther changes were called for. Commissioners were appointed for enquiring into the goods, bells etc. of all

Churches and Chapels. Sir Tho. Gyfford and Sir Tho. Fitzherbert knts. and Walter Wrottesley, Esq., in Staffordsh., took the inventory for Tamworth Oct. 7th in the same year, and found, "Fyrste iij belles, iij Sacrynge belles;" and the articles left in 1548; and for the Chapel of Wigginton there remained there, "ij Smale bells, one vestement w^t the appurten'ncs." Two bells not as yet taken from the steeple of the Church had been sold with the assent of the whole Parish to Tho. Endsore and Rob. Growtwiche for 10*l.* "to be employed & bestowed vpon the Free schole & other necessaryes of the Churche and Towne now soore in decay."

Three Commissioners, being Walter Viscount Hereford Lord Ferrers of Chartley, Sir Tho. Fitzherbert, and Edw. Littleton, Esq. the next May 14th delivered to Hen. Seale and John Wodshawe, Churchwardens,

    " ij chaleses of Siluer wth patents,

    v belles in the Stepull,

    ij linen Clothes ffor the holli co'union table,

    a Surples ffor the curat to minestre in,"

safely to be kept till the king's pleasure was farther known. These were all the articles that were now needed for the new Church Service, the rest went to the Crown. It seems as if the sale of the two bells had been set aside; for then the difference of the two statements as to the number of bells is at once cleared up.

The church-property of Tamworth speedily passed from the Crown into private hands. The lands etc. belonging to the obits of Tho. Meire and Rich. Dalton, Humf. Jacob, and Peter Goabowt, and the land in Wigginton (now occupied by Edw. Broks) for Tho. Wright's second obit, were rated Dec. 6th 1548 for Rich. Goodriche of London, but were sold Mar. 28th 1549 to Hen. Tanner and Tho. Bocher of London. Edward VI. made a more sweeping sale July 21st following to Rog. Alford and Geo. Harryson gents. and Tho. Burnet citizen and barber of London, including the old possessions for the support of the Morrow Mass Priest and Schoolmaster held by Tho. Aynsworth, John Colman, Will. Michell, John Blodeworth, Humf. Torre, *Rich. Broke*, John Chare and John Aynsworth; the lands etc. of the obits of John Geffrey, John à Grene, and Rich. Baxter; of Bailey's endowment for the Schoolmaster, the lands etc. held by Hen. Alred, Rog. Wright, Tho. Bek, Agnes Botte, Will. Coton, Rob. Melbourne, and Rich. Cowper; the possessions of the obits of Will. Akeyley, John Mathewe, John Price and Leonard Ferrers, John Seale, Hen. Cowper, and Tho. Tayler; and again of the old endowment for the St. George Priest, the messuages etc. held by John Hewer, Will. Edes, and Rob. Bucknell. Wigginton Chapel with the burial-ground was sold at the same time to Alford and Harryson: Fazeley Free Chapel and Chapelyard Dec. 22nd to Sir John Peryent knt. and Tho. Reve; whilst Fazeley water-mill belonging to it and the cottage called "the Prestes Chambre" with its adjoining garden and curtilage went Feb. 8th following to Hugh Wyatt. And July 11th 1550 the king sold to Walt. and Edw. Leveson gents., the garden and lands for the two Chapels in the Church in the tenure of Lawr. Damport, and the messuage for the Schoolmaster in that of John Sponer. The king Mar. 29th 1551 leased, for twenty-one years from the last Ladyday at the yearly rent of 104*l.* 6*s.* 5*d.*, the Deanery and Prebends with the Rectory of Middleton to Michael Camswell gent., who acted as bailiff of the Crown till his death early in 1561.

It is seen above that the School House and garden were sold. Richard Broke became Minister here: he conformed in Mary's time, but ceased it would seem rather than change again when Elizabeth commanded it.

Under the ecclesiastical restoration of queen Mary no change was made in the new form of the establishment at Tamworth. But one or more of the altars being set up again, the ancient liturgy and rites were brought back. Some legal hitch took place as to the Schoolmaster's salary, which the Receiver General of Staffordsh. (the Court of Augmentations being abolished) refused to pay from Michaelmas 1555. Richard Broke appealed to the Court of Exchequer; and it was ordered June 13th 1558 that he and his successors should still have the stipend of 10l. 13s. 2$\frac{1}{2}d$. and all arrears were to be paid.

In the time of Philip and Mary the Parish Register was first begun Mar. 4th 1556-7.

The Reformation was settled at last on the country by Elizabeth, who enforced the Book of Common Prayer from June 24th 1559. Here a Communion Table again took the place of the High Altar at the east end of the Chancel. This queen disposed of the rest of the church-property. In paying the debts of the Duke of Somerset (executed for high-treason in Edward's time) she granted Aug. 25th 1562 to Cicily widow of John Pickerell gent., treasurer and cofferer of the Duke's household, all those lands etc. at Tamworth in both counties in the occupation of — Ferrers gent., and the 10a. of land in the occupation of the Churchwardens and others, which had been concealed and withheld from the Crown. Also Dec. 18th 1563 she sold to Will. Grice, Esq., and Anthony Forster of Cumnor in Berksh., the barn and croft (in the tenure of Margaret Barnaby widow) left for the Mass of our Lady of Grace, the two cottages in Lichfield St. (held by Geo. Grafton) for the yearly obit, and Pristley Fields and Pristly Riddings. Rich. Robson gent. bought Martin's Croft, Feb. 1st following, then in the tenure of John Jeks, and of the clear yearly value of 13s. The Prebend of Wilnecote was leased

June 27th 1570 to Ralph Burton and Rich. Repington, for twenty-one years from the last Ladyday, at the rent of 14*l*. 6*s*. 8*d*.

The search after withheld and concealed church-property was eagerly pursued by greedy adventurers who prowled up and down all the country. Amongst them one Rob. Hurleston claimed reward from the queen for his industry in finding some houses and lands at his own trouble and expence, in Rugeley, *Baymoo grene*, Tamworth, Bloxwich, Walsall, and Shawbury in Shropsh., worth altogether 70*s*. 8*d*. a-year. His grand discovery at Tamworth consisted of the well-known *College howse* and garden of the late Vicars in *Cockett Lane* tenanted by John Mounforde for 13*s*. 4*d*. So July 2nd 1567 he got a lease of all he had found, for twenty-one years from the last Ladyday at the same rate as the existing rents. It was perhaps best not to be too strict with such useful fellows in noticing all their petty frauds.

By letters-patent dated October 27th 1581 Elizabeth granted to Edmund Downing and Peter Ashton *inter alia* all the late College, and the Deanery, and the Prebends of Wigginton, Bonehill, Wilnecote, Coton, and Syerscote; with all buildings, lands, glebes, commons, tithes, oblations, and emoluments; and the advowson and right of patronage of the Vicarage and Church. These were to be held as of the Manor of East Greenwich, by fealty, in free soccage, at the yearly rent of 33*l*. 13*s*. 2½*d*. to the Crown; also of 62*l*. 0*s*. 5½*d*. in sums of 18*s*. 1*d*. for the Archdeacon's synodals and proxies, 22*s*. 6*d*. for the Bishop's perpetual pension, 20*l*. for the Vicar's and 16*l*. for the two Curates' stipends, 10*l*. 13*s*. 2½*d*. for the Schoolmaster's salary, and 13*l*. 6*s*. 8*d*. for the stipend of the Curate of Tatenhill. Downing and Ashton Feb. 21st 1582-3 passed the whole to John Morley and Rog. Rant. And in a very short time Morley and Rant (who was his servant) sold out the whole in parcels. They granted the Deanery or Prebend of Amington and the Prebend of Wigginton with the tithes belonging May 10th 1583 to Thomas Repington, Esq., of Amington; also the advowson and patronage of the Vicarage and Church. The Prebend of Bonehill was sold to Will. Necton, Wilnecote to Geo. Corbin, Coton to Alex. Morley, and Syerscote to John Breton.

And again Jan. 19th 1581-2 the queen granted to Edw. Froste gent. and John Walker, all the temporal lands and hereditaments in Staffordsh. and Warwicksh., which yet remained of the late College. The rent out of Claverley Mill for Sir Thomas Ferrers' obit was still paid in 1608 to the Crown by the Lord of Tamworth Castle; we have not sought out its later history. The Rectory of Middleton was sold to Willoughby, lord of that Manor.

But in her charter to the Town Oct. 10th 1588

Elizabeth granted to the Bailiffs and Capital Burgesses (or Corporate Body) of Tamworth the ancient fair of St. Edith, now called St. Swithen's Fair; and gave them as Guardians and Governors of the Free Grammar School the appointment of the Preacher and two Curates, subject to the approval of the High Steward of the Borough.

We might tell how St. Swithen's Fair was claimed by the purchasers of the Prebends, but was adjudged to the Corporation because it was not named in the grant to Downing and Ashton; how amidst many other wearisome strifes at law, long, rankling, and costly dissensions arose between the family of Repington and the Guardians of the School, which ran on for nigh two hundred years before they were settled; and (though we do not follow Spelman's fancies) how the property of the Prebends has passed through ever-varying hands, and through fine old families which are now for the most part unremembered in the country around. But these interesting matters belong to the history of the modern Parish Church of Tamworth. And that history needs a book to itself.

It is hard to discover how the inhabitants of Tamworth took to the several changes of religion in the middle of the sixteenth century, when decay too smote the town, a *sore* decay indeed, for within three years a third of the adult population disappeared from the Parish. Nearly all the records of the Borough for that period perished by fire or have been lost. At the great Court of the Staffordshire side held Oct. 21st 1550 the following penalty was imposed: "It' pe' y^t no ma' shall Receve no ma' in to ther howssys att s'uice tyme, s'b pe' iij$^{s.}$ iiij$^{d.}$, halff to the balies, & the other to the com' bocks." And in the next Court Apr. 27th 1551 Will. Wodde was amerced in 12d. "for keping of s'vaunts at y^e s'monde tyme." Of the eleven members of the College who were pensioned in 1548, four died within eight years, but in the beginning of 1556 Johnson, Horton, Synger, Pyndar, Hatherington, Baddesley, and Lesset were still enjoying their pay. The last dignitaries and incumbents of the ancient Collegiate Church of Tamworth seem to have fallen in with every shifting humour of their royal head in Henry's and Edward's times, and to have taken up the old faith again whilst Mary held the throne. Herein all can pity but none may justify them. And thus perhaps it went on till death swept the hirelings away. Even the Dean's house soon vanished in a winding-sheet of fire which wrapped half the town in swift destruction.

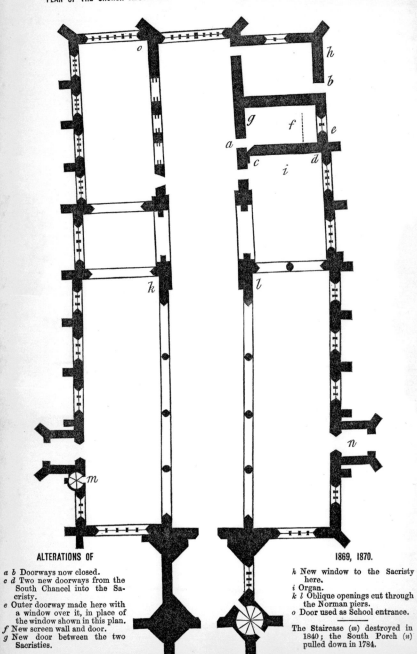

PLAN OF THE CHURCH ABOUT 1760.

Scale—10 yards to the inch.

ALTERATIONS OF   1869, 1870.

a b Doorways now closed.
c d Two new doorways from the
    South Chancel into the Sa-
    cristy.
e Outer doorway made here with
    a window over it, in place of
    the window shown in this plan.
f New screen wall and door.
g New door between the two
    Sacristies.

h New window to the Sacristy
    here.
i Organ.
k l Oblique openings cut through
    the Norman piers.
o Door used as School entrance.

The Staircase (*m*) destroyed in
    1840; the South Porch (*n*)
    pulled down in 1784.

CHAPTER VI.

ANCIENT CHURCH, CHURCHYARD, DEAN'S HOUSE ETC., AND STONE CROSS.

Church.

THE buildings of the ancient Church consisted of a Choir, North and South Transepts, Nave, North and South Aisles each with a Porch, and a Tower at the W. end of the Nave. On the N. side of the Choir the Chantry Chapel of St. George, on the S. a room which we suppose to have been a greater Sacristy, and between it and the Transept a Smaller Sacristy. Beneath the South Aisle a Crypt Chapel.

The following are the interior

DIMENSIONS OF THE CHURCH.

Choir	Length, 48½ ft.	Breadth, 23½ ft.
Between the Transepts	„ 30¼ „	„ 22½ „
North Transept... ...	„ 18 „	„ 25½ „
South Transept	„ 35½ „	„ 24¾ „
Nave	„ 76½ „	„ 24 „
North Aisle	„ 78½ „	„ 26¼ „
South Aisle	„ 81 „	„ 26½ „
North Porch	„ 10½ „	„ 10½ „

South Porch	... ...	Length,	10½ ft.	Breadth,	10½ ft.
Tower...		„	21 „	„	21 „
Chantry Chapel of St.					
George		„	52½ „	„	23¾ „
Greater Sacristy ...		„	17½ „	„	24¼ „
Smaller Sacristy... ...		„	13½ „	„	24¼ „
Crypt Chapel		„	56¾ „	„	16¼ „

The present fabric shows in its architecture that the Church was built at different periods. Between the Transepts on either side stands a massive semicircular stilted arch above thirteen feet in span with indented and lozenge-shaped mouldings all in the oldest Norman style of the eleventh century. The lower parts of the N. and S. walls of the Choir seem to be quite as ancient. In the S. wall just E. of the large arch a doorway and above it a window both round-headed have all the marks of the same epoch.

Hence it appears that the Church was built again soon after the Conquest, most likely in the reign of William Rufus; and that it was cruciform, having a Tower between the Choir, Transepts, and Nave. Perhaps the Nave had Side Aisles.

The Crypt underneath two-thirds of the length and breadth of the South Aisle and reaching to its E. end is in a much later style. It is built of rag-stone, vaulted and groined, and is divided into four compartments or bays by octagonal piers half sunk in the wall. These piers each support segmental groining ribs of a similar form, which pass longitudinally, transversely, and diagonally. The doorway into the Crypt with a semi-circular head: two simple splayed openings for windows on the S. side. The entrance was from the Churchyard at the Porch, the surface of the soil outside being then some feet below the present level, till 1784, when the South Porch was pulled down and a narrow brick passage into the Crypt was made from the Aisle above in place of the

Crypt of the Church.

ancient outer doorway. At the E. end of the Crypt the remains of the Altar. This was *the Chapel in the Churchyard* which we have already mentioned. When it ceased to be a Chapel it was used for the bones accidentally cast up in digging graves, and became about two-thirds filled with those grim relics of the dead piled up in decent order.

The two Sacristies built of ragstone have been so thoroughly debased that it is hard to fix a date for them; each was entered from the Choir by a doorway with the square-headed trefoil arch of the twelfth and three following centuries. In later times the larger Sacristy was turned into a lumber-room, and the doorway into the Chancel was bricked up, an entrance being made on the S. side. The doorway into the Chancel was re-opened in 1853. The Smaller Sacristy became the Vestry. The whole externally has been re-faced with stone.

When the Church was restored after the fire of 1345 the equilateral pointed arch was brought in. The greater part of the building must be set down to that period. The Nave separated from the Aisle on each side by four arches supported by piers formed of four semicylindrical shafts united together, with corresponding plain moulded capitals and bases. Each Aisle with four windows and a porch-door at the side and a W. window, and marked off from the adjoining Transept, the North Aisle by one arch, the South Aisle by two smaller arches. The North Transept with a large window, and separated from a chapel on the E. by an arch. The South Transept lengthened eastwards so as to form chapels, lighted by two windows on the S. and a large one at the E. end. The Choir raised by adding three windows on each side above the Norman parts of the wall left standing, three cinquefoiled arches made beneath these windows on the N. opening into a chapel, and a W. window.

The Freviles doubtless lent a generous hand in restoring the Choir, for it was the burial-place of the Lords of the Castle. We have a fair presumption too but no sure warrant for believing that Edward III. aided the work. We might have found a certainty in this if the great fire had happened a few years earlier. For the royal alms under strict rules of court-routine were so abundant that the records of them form a clue to where the king was as he went about from place to place. But in the middle of Edward's reign during the fierce struggle for the mastery of France, these alms became abated except as private gifts doled out infrequently. The royal path is then no longer tracked by the golden thread of charity, but is left to be sought along the thick blood-drops of war and the land-marks of political events. The North Transept has been all along called the Comberford Chapel : to that family the building of it is traditionally ascribed, and there they had their sepulture.

The original architectural details of these parts of the building are much changed or obscured. The five buttresses of the North Aisle are modern, those W. of the Porch being rebuilt in 1840, when the face of intervening walls was chiselled over, the W. wall and window of the same Aisle also undergoing the same treatment. The exterior of the South Aisle was refaced with stone in 1784, when the five buttresses too were rebuilt, and the North Transept was likewise renewed. The South Transept was rough-chisselled about the same time as the North Aisle; the E. window has been built up, so that the raised roof of the Vestry might rest against it.

The Tower is massive, and has four square turrets with spires at the corners. The spires seem to have been once much shorter than they are now, and to have been also ornamented with crockets, and perhaps with finials before weather-cocks were put up. Between them is a large octagonal basement which it is believed was for a large middle spire, but was capped over and left unfinished. At the S.E. angle of the Tower the buttress of the turret runs into the W. wall of the Aisle. But at the N.E. angle the buttress en-croaches over the W. window of the North Aisle, and in order to lose as little light as possible the lowest stage of the buttress was made less in width from the window-sill upwards than the rest of the tower buttresses. This shows that the Tower was built after the Aisle.

Although three large windows were made in it, the Tower had great strength and many arrange-ments of a defensive fortress. There are passages in the walls and small rooms in the turrets, all pierced with loop-holes which command the open

Double Staircase.

sides of the Tower. The Church had regular watchmen. In the Court-Leet of the Staffordsh. side of the town held Oct. 2nd 1329, it was presented that hue had been raised and blood shed between John le Cartwrytth, Rob. his brother, Rich. Tocke, and Will. son of Will. Symond, and the watchmen of the Church and of the town, in the night: these four were amerced, and they would not suffer themselves to be arrested.

The Staircase in the S.W. turret of the Tower is very curious, and shows a piece of architecture which is very seldom met with even abroad. Two flights of steps wind one above the other round the same newel, so that the floor of the one forms the roof of the other, all enclosed within a cylinder six feet in diameter and lighted from without by loopholes. One person may go up and another down the Tower at the same time without meeting. The engraving gives a better and clearer idea of this structure than a long description could do. One flight of steps begins in the Churchyard at a doorway, above which was once an image in a large canopied niche. About two-thirds up these stairs is a blind passage in the S. wall, where three large splayed loopholes with trefoiled heads overlook the town, Castle, and surrounding country. The stairs, of 106 steps, then end a little above the door to the top of the Tower. These stairs would have been very useful if the Tower was designed for beacon-fires and signals in times of

9

trouble and warfare. The other flight begins at a plain doorway within the Tower and leads into all the rooms. By a small doorway to a room in the N.W. turret, along a narrow path in front of the W. window. This room like the others of the same sort in the Tower is about 5 ft. square, with three loopholes for light, and groined roofs. Higher up the stairs, a passage in the wall lighted with two square apertures, to another of the small rooms, and two doorways from the passage into the ringers' room. Higher the entrance into the Belfry. Still higher up a doorway overlooking the Belfry. And then these stairs, of 101 steps, end at the door at the top of the Tower.

In the N.E. corner of the ringers' room is a doorway into one of the small rooms, and thence a passage with two loopholes in the E. wall to another room. In the N. wall of the ringers' room a recess lighted by a large trefoil-headed opening. From the E. side of this recess a flight of stone steps in the wall runs from some distance down towards the roof of the North Aisle: Near the bottom of these stairs a passage of steps in the S. wall turns up to a door in the valley of the early high-pitched roof of the Nave, but now leading out on the top of the body of the Church; then down again, and at last eastward towards the roof of the South Aisle. The Belfry, square below octagonal above, has eight simple-pointed windows, two on each side; and in each corner is one of the small rooms, here somewhat octagonal as the masonry is not so massive as below.

Part of the parapet of the Tower on the E. side, sheltered by the S.E. pinnacle is built into two square piers. An altar-stone might have rested upon them. This is a bold conjecture for a curious variation in the form of the battlements wherein historical evidence fails and no other explanation is easily given. The narrow way around the central basement for a spire suggests that temporary altar-steps were used; at least all traces of fixed ones must have disappeared in later repairs of the tower-leads. At certain seasons Mass might have been celebrated there under the broad canopy of heaven, commemorating Him who is typified by the bright and morning star. Such a service aloft is still shadowed forth on the tower of Magdalen College, Oxford, at day-break of the first of May, when the choristers chant the Eucharistic Hymn and sing in Flora's honour, till within late years amidst showers of rotten eggs for luckless heads below, with the harsh braying of May-horns. This ceremonial took the place of a Requiem for the soul of Henry VII. It would indeed be interesting if we could discover that this king bestowed royal largess towards the alterations of this Church, and had his commemoration at Tamworth too. He had good cause to regard this town favourably in recalling the time when he was simply Earl of

Richmond the adventurer on his route towards Bosworth battle-field, where the crown of England was set upon his head. For after leaving Lichfield Aug. 18th 1485 he lost his way in the dusk of evening, and only joined his troops again next morning at Tamworth, where he rode publicly through the streets to allay the alarm of his followers at his sudden and unseasonable disappearrance. This interesting episode in the Wars of the Roses is narrated by several writers within a century after it happened; amongst them by one at the royal court who wrote at Henry VII.'s command, and by another who dwelt in the neighbourhood of Tamworth and surely would not have departed from the local tradition when folk-lore was still a trusty guide in history.

The Tower has undergone many modern changes. The stone ceiling of the entrance was destroyed and a ringers' room entered by a passage from the outer staircase was formed below the old one. In 1849 this lower room was removed, the ceiling restored, and the old ringers' room used again. The staircase being much worn was also mostly rebuilt, but at the same time the doorway to the passage in front of the W. window was stopped. The mullions of the Belfry windows rebuilt. The pinnacles have been thrown down in part several times during storms or gales and as often repaired. None of the six bells are ancient, as they bear the dates of 1672, 1621, 1629, 1628, 1656, and 1607.

The North Porch has been very much defaced so that its architectural features are nearly lost. The entrance-arch seems to have had an ogee canopy; and above it, ornamented with crockets and finial but now nearly plastered up was

—— " a little Gothic niche
Of nicest workmanship; that once had held
The sculptured image of some patron Saint,
Or of the Blessed Virgin, looking down
On all who entered those religious doors."—*Wordsworth.*

The Porch vaulted and groined. Above the entrance a room without a fireplace, lighted by two round openings in the N. wall, and with an ogee loophole into the Aisle. Up to it from the Aisle an ogee doorway on the W. side of the Porch, a small spiral staircase in the buttress, and a passage in the wall. The doorway in the Aisle had been built up for a long time, and in 1840 the staircase was destroyed when the buttress was rebuilt, although the room remains, which might have served for a chaplain or a sacristan. This Porch formed one of the entrances into the Church until 1809.

The South Porch was pulled down in 1784 and the entrance into the Church from it built up. According to an old plan and the recollections of some ancient inhabitants of the Town gleaned nigh forty years ago, this Porch was like the one on the N. side, but without a room above the entrance.

The last great change in the architectural features of the old Church was in the time of the Tudors, mostly with the four-centred depressed arch. The roofs had hitherto been high-pitched. The form of the first roofs is still traced on the E. wall and buttresses of the Tower for the Nave and Aisles; and on the E. wall of the South Transept and by corbels in the walls for that part of the building, where the roof ran longitudinally from E. to W. and opposite the Norman arch was met by another transverse roof. But now a clerestory was formed all along the body of the Church, and the roofs except those of the Porches were made flat. In the clerestory on each side of the Nave six windows with a shallow canopied panel and a moulded bracket for an image betwixt: above the Transept arches and along the Choir seven windows (the first three] eastern ones simple pointed) also with panelled niches. This change needed all the gables except the E. one of the South Transept to be built again, and so the E. window of the Choir with a niche for an image and a canopied panel above on each side was made new, and also the W. windows of the two Aisles. The three large windows with panelled jambs and arches in the Tower, one into the Nave above the doorway, another in the S. wall, and the third on the W. side above the principal doorway, all matched with the fine elliptical groined ceiling of the entrance, and are remarkable specimens of their era : the tracery of the S. window was renewed in 1844 in the perpendicular style. The Chantry Chapel of St. George was built on the site of the more ancient one, with four windows and buttresses on the N. side, and a large E. window with a canopied niche and bracket sculptured into a cherub for an image, on each side.

The window-tracery of the clerestory is not old. In the summer of 1837 the South clerestory of the Nave was wholly refaced with stone and the windows repaired with new mullions, but the small buttresses between the windows were left out altogether. None of the roofs are more than two hundred years old. Those of the Chancel and Nave were put up in 1807. The roof of the North Aisle bears the date 1731, but much of the ancient materials was used again; and that of the South Aisle 1671. The flooring of the Church was all renewed in 1809.

Some parts of the Church were used for public meetings concerning the government of the Town, probably the Aisles near the Porches, and for the religious plays or Mysteries which were common in the middle ages. At the Court Leet of the Staffordsh. side Apr. 29th 1372, it was ordered, with the assent of the Frankpledgers, that they should go every other week to the Church, to *le Brother mosse* on the Monday, there to ordain and amend the constitutions at their Great Court; and none to leave out doing so under penalty of 3s. 4d. The Brother Mass might have been connected with the Guild of St. George. Early in the reign of Henry VI. two common halls (one for each side of the town) were in use, and then only petty meetings took place in the Church. The Staffordsh. Court Leet Oct. 18th 1516 records a pain put on all the tenants of the town, that they should not gather money at the services or plays in the Church nor in the town under penalty of 3s. 4d., 20d. to go to the Church and 20d. to the Bailiffs.

A complaint in the Star Chamber has some curious charges against Sir Humfrey Ferrers. His father Sir John Ferrers was the High Steward of Tamworth during the royal pleasure by grant of Henry VII. Jan. 29th, 1506-7; but the office was given by Henry VIII. Nov. 25th 1510 to Walter Devereux, lord Ferrers of Chartley, for life. Sir Humfrey Ferrers too became High Steward, but we have failed to discover how he was appointed. Lord Ferrers (then Viscount Hereford) did not die till 1558. Rivalry for the honour of being governor and leader of the military levies of this town, which was the chief duty of the Stewardship, led Sir Humfrey to overstep the powers of the office in other matters, and created grievances with the Bailiffs which made them egg on one of the Serjeants-at-Mace against him. Will. Bett the Serjeant charged him with an assault in the Church, and with assaulting others particularly a man in a Mystery acted here. What took place is gathered in our narrative from the examinations of many witnesses taken Jan. 18th 1536-7 at Tamworth.

Lawrence Damport one of the High Bailiffs of the Staffordshire side was in the Church with Bett on Relic Sunday (July 9th) 1536 after Even-song, giving the bakers the assize of bread for the following week. Then Sir Humfrey Ferrers having with him only Tho. Swynnerton Sir John Griffith's servant (though on the other side it was declared that he had four servants, two of them with swords and bucklers) came down the Church and took Bett to task for not attending him as High Steward, according to custom in the great procession of that day, saying, "S'jant, what is the cause that thow woldyst not wayte apon me, as thy duty was, in p'cessyon? Wher were ye, this day?" Bett said that he was with his masters, and when Sir Humfrey asked who were his masters answered, "Master Jeyks and Lawrence Damport," meaning the two High Bailiffs. Angry words soon stirred up fury. Bett said Sir Humfrey should command those to wait upon him to whom he gave meat and drink, that himself was bound to wait upon the Bailiffs, and that the king's grace or Sir Humfrey or my Lord Ferrers had nought to do within the same town, as the king had granted all his privileges to the

10

Bailiffs. On hearing this Sir Humfrey exclaimed,
"Avaunt, knave, wottest thow what thow say-
est?" And he gave him a *lytell lyke* or slap on
the cheek with the back of his hand, crying out,
"Ye horeson knave, I shall teche bothe the & thi
masters to wayte apon me." Bett retorted, "If
my masters do so comand me I wyll so do, orels
I wyll not." Then Sir Humfrey threatened that
if he had him out of the Church he would stick a
dagger into him. Bett dared him to do so.
Thereupon Sir Humfrey *covetyd* to strike him
with his dagger. But Rob. Gretwyche one of
the High Bailiffs of the Warwickshire side stepped
in, saying, "S^r, at the reu'ance of God, remember
wher ye ar." Sir Humfrey rejoined, "I wot
wher I am aswell as thow." Damport also hindered him with fair words from using his weapon;
and so going out of the Church with a last threat
to Bett, "Well, horeson, I wyll trym the," Sir
Humfrey went home to the Castle. Next day
at the desire of Lady Ferrers Sir Humfrey's
wife, Gretwyche waited on the fiery knight and
advertized him to keep the king's peace, and Sir
Humfrey yielded to do so. Bett owned that the
blow neither felled him nor put him into any
jeopardy of his life.

Nor was the other assault a very grave affair.
A play was acted on Corpus Christi-day (June
15th) in the same year, and Will. Toke alias
Johnson twenty-one years old servant to Will.

Tarre acted the devil, having great iron chains about him. Sir Humfrey Ferrers was amongst those gazing on, and Toke (Sir Humfrey said wrongly it was Tarre who was devil) going rudely by unwarily struck him with the chains and broke his shins. Sir Humfrey being displeased cried out, "I beshrow thy hert," and said to his servants wishing them to give the fellow a box or two on the ears, "Is ther none of yowe that wyll gyve him a blowe?" His servant Anderson went up to *devil* and asked him why he thus hurt his master with the chain. The man replied, "Why, knave, he myght have stoude forther out my way then." Anderson having such a *lewde* answer struck him with his dagger and broke his head in two places, but no greater harm was done.

In most collegiate churches there was no chancel-arch, and at Tamworth a Rood screen must have marked off the Choir from the body of the Church. The Choir had stalls and sedilia all perhaps with many a grotesque figure carved with curious art, though no trace of them is now left. The broken piscina is still in the S. wall near where the High Altar stood. The Church was certainly a very fine one and was made befitting that Presence without which it would have been for the most part only a pleasing but useless and costly toy. The relics still left and records of what has been, go far to pourtray the building about the year 1520 in the heyday of its glory, and let us catch a glimpse of what it was, yet like the memory of a dream that denies to the pencil the details which the imagination alone depicts. The fine chisel of the sculptor has given bold outline and nice tracery to altars, arches, windows, corbels, niches, and images of Saints and Angels. The skilful brush of the limner has shed over all rich glowing hues and quaintly set forth some scripture-history or old legend. Here and there ever-burning lamps are twinkling. The windows are filled with stained glass and

> Through tinctur'd shapes of saints and kings
> The shafted sun-beams smile,

decking the tesselated pavements with party-colours which creep athwart the graves and monuments and fling bright halos on the dead, then ripple up the storied walls and vanish with the waning day.

There were several altars within the Church. The Altar of the Most Holy Trinity and St. Edith in the Choir. The Altar of the Blessed Virgin Mary at the E. end of the South Aisle perhaps in wooden parcloses, and in all likelihood the Image of our Lady in the N.E. corner on the fine panelled pedestal of stone once bedeckt with gold and paint. The Altar of St. George at the E. end of the Chantry Chapel. The Altar of St. Nicholas in the South Transept, and to the left of it or in the North Transept that of St. Katherine the Martyr. The Light of the Most Holy Trinity and the Lights of these Saints fell under the care of chief inhabitants of the town who were elected yearly to the charge in autumn-tide at the great Court. These Wardens of the Lights took oath to fulfil the duties of their office in gathering alms and taking the rents of the endowments for the purpose, so that they might trim their lamps and keep them always shining.

The niches, brackets and pedestals throughout the building show that there were many sculptured figures. In the Choir stood the Image of St. Edith. Each roof perhaps had embellishments of the same kind all fashioned out of wood. Within our own memory, in the North Aisle to each of the six tie-beams the wall-plate with a spandrell serving as a brace had a large demi-angel in alb, stole, and girdle, but these bold carvings were taken down more than thirty years ago. The dripstone corbels outside some of the windows in the North clerestory of the present Chancel have fine half-length forms of clerks in cope or alb all now in sad decay.

Beneath three centuries of whitewash are still found traces of the colouring which decorated the Choir and all the Chapels even the Crypt. But the subjects or patterns on the walls could be very imperfectly made out now, and only at a trouble and cost which would not be duly paid back, so often has the building been daubed and patched and changed and daubed again. Twenty-five years ago we discovered large paintings (24 ft. by 11 ft.) on all the E. wall of the South Transept from the floor to the stringcourse beneath the window. We carefully traced them before the mason's brush at last blotted them out for ever. The subject on the right-hand half of the wall was painted on the stone in Edward III's time. In the centre a blank space plastered where the Image of St. Nicholas must have stood under a canopy. To the right of the image on a dark red ground three nude demi-figures of tonsured clerics rising out of a tub, according to the legend which says that this Bishop of Myra raised to life three students who had been secretly murdered and hidden in a meal-barrel. To the left of the image also on a red ground three females in long white gowns and wimples kneeling in prayer towards the Saint, in all likelihood figures of three ladies who caused the image and painting to be made. To the whole a back-ground diapered in horizontal rows of large vermilion and green lozenges, the white fret-work having black lozenges at the crossings and in each vermilion lozenge a gilt crescent. The figures and countenances of the females seemed to pourtray the successive ages of sisters. Now in all the abundant records of this town in Edward III.'s time, we have found only once just three sisters and having means to give freely towards restoring the Church. Edith, Constance, and Alice, daughters of John de Bollenhull of Tamworth draper and Alice his wife, were of a fair ancestry which flourished at Bollenhull, or Bonehill, till the crime of fratricide and flight of the murderer blasted its honour. Alexander de Bollenhull slew his brother Geoffrey at Bonehill June 19th 1325, and was outlawed at Tamworth, for the Staffordshire as well as the Warwickshire Assizes were often held here before the ruinous fire of 1345. A branch of the family also dwelt at Dunstall. The sisters are mentioned in 1349 as heiresses to an entail, in case their only brother John died without issue. Thus we risk a mere likelihood to identify the females in the painting. On the window-sill of the first S. window close by is fixed a small hexagonal pedestal with quatrefoils on three sides and at the base the letters R N, perhaps for an image or a light.

The painting on the other half of the wall was on plaster and dated about the close of the fifteenth century. In the middle on a red ground a Crucifixion with Mary and John. To this a back-ground of four arches four-centred and depressed with crockets and finials, the first and last arch being smaller than the others. The subjects in the first, third and fourth compartments were destroyed, except in the third a hand in benediction and some fragments of figures.

Under the second arch on a green ground a female kneeling at an altar, on the edge of which her joined hands rested. Close by her an alb-clothed figure holding in his right hand a crozier which passed betwixt her arms, and in his left a book. A mitre on the altar, a benedictory hand in the arch above. The Life of St. Edith might have been told here. The artists of these two pieces certainly had not the gifted touch of the great Dominican painter Fra Angelico da Fiesole to light up the countenances of the figures with wondrous beams of holiness and joy, still they gave a pleasing page to teach unlettered folks and raise their thoughts above the world.

When these paintings were defaced at the Reformation some mottoes were written up where they had been. We strove to recover these wise sentences, but could only just catch the words in black letter "thow that" and "feign" as the deepest layer of whitewash crumbled beneath our hand. The wall ceased to be for the poor; it appealed no longer to the lowly heart and addressed the educated intellect alone. But truly that was an age of respectability, when the pews were first brought in here to

"Screen the rich burgher from the vulgar dunce."

In the Crypt Chapel opposite the first window from the entrance was another painting now completely lost, which was also replaced by an inscription in Latin verse.

O *dom*inus dives
Non om*n*i *tem*pore vives,
Fac b*ene* du*m* vivis
Post morte*m* viv*er*e si vis.
M*iserer*e Jesu Chris*t*e.

Fragments of stained glass have been found in digging graves within the Church. In 1844 a hand in benediction, part of a tonsured head, and some floreal pieces were turned up in opening a vault in the old Vestry. A few notices remain of the subjects once in the windows. Notes taken "At the parishe church of Tamworthe, 1590," give the following arms.

Gu. 3 lions passant guardant Or; on a label of 3 points Az. 9 fleurs-de-liz of the second. [Plantagenet.]

Arg. on a chief Az. 2 estoiles of 6 points Or. [Clinton of Maxtoke.]

Gu. a lion rampant Or.

Or 3 chevronells Gu. [Clare.]

Az. a cross patoncé between 4 martlets Or.

Az. a bend cotized Arg. between 6 lions rampant Or (Bohun).

Warren. [Chequy Or and Sa.]

Plantagenet. Basset of Blore. [Gu. 3 bars wavy Or.] Frevile, Baldwin. [Or a cross flory Gu.] Ferrers de Groby. [Gu. 7 mascles conjoined, 3, 3, and 1, Or.] England and France. Stafford. Plantagenet.

Beauchamp. [Gu. a fess between 6 cross-croslets Or.]

To these Wyrley's Church Notes in 1597, printed in Shaw's History of Staffordshire, add the following.

Basset of Drayton. [Or 3 piles Gu., a canton Ermine.]

Arg. 3 bars Az. with a label of 3 points Or.

Az. 3 crowns Or, 2 and 1.

. . . . A border of fleurs-de-liz.

Vairy Arg. and Az. a fess Or with a . . . . . . indented Gu.

Fretty Arg. and Sa.

Or on a bend cotized Vert 3 mullets Gu. [*sic.*]

Or a saltire engrailed Sa. [Botetourt.]

Gu. on a cross engrailed Or five roses of the first [Comberford] impaling, party per pale indented Or and Az.

Arms for "Johannes Ferrers miles & Mat . . .

da . . . or d'na Dorothea ux . . . p'fat Jo. Harpur."

And for " Johannes Ferrers mil. fil. Tho. Ferrers, Anna ux. fil . . . Hastings mil. & Matild. fil. Stanley 2 ux."

"Johannes Ferrers & Doro. ux. ejus obiit 1512."

" These armes of the Ferrers were soe broken, and withal so badly made, that the truth thereof could not be well discerned."

Not fifty years afterwards Dugdale mentions only two pieces of stained glass and gives engravings of them. One in the E. window of the Chancel depicted the grant of the Castle to Robert le Marmion, and under it was written:

𝔥𝔦𝔠 𝔭𝔢𝔯 𝔚𝔦𝔩𝔩𝔦𝔢𝔩𝔪𝔲𝔪 𝔠𝔬𝔫𝔮𝔲𝔢𝔰𝔱𝔬𝔯𝔢𝔪 𝔯𝔬𝔟𝔢𝔯𝔱𝔲𝔰 𝔪𝔞𝔯𝔪𝔦𝔬𝔫 𝔡𝔬𝔪𝔦𝔫𝔲𝔰 𝔠𝔞𝔰𝔱𝔢𝔩𝔩𝔦 𝔢𝔣𝔣𝔦𝔠𝔦𝔱𝔲𝔯.

The second piece was " in a north window : " a knight and four sons, a lady and three daughters, all kneeling in prayer; with the fragment of an inscription below,

. . . . 𝔣𝔢𝔯𝔯𝔢𝔯𝔰 𝔪𝔦𝔩𝔦𝔱𝔦𝔰 . . . . . 𝔢𝔱 𝔡'𝔫𝔞 𝔡𝔬𝔯𝔬𝔱𝔥𝔢𝔞 . . .

On his surcoat the arms: quarterly, 1st Ferrers of Groby with a label of 3 points; 2nd Botetourt; 3rd Frevile; 4th Mountford. Upon the mantle of Lady Dorothy Ferrers nearly the same arms, with those of Harper additional.

When Thomas visited the Church in 1730 all these were gone. In our own time there were only two ancient pieces of stained glass, very small and nearly out of view in the right side of the E. window of the Chancel. A skull and under it a coffin marked with a cross and placed upon a trestle. Along the sides short scrolls inscribed,

Mors	et	Judisiu'
Vesca		vermiu'
Nosce		te ip'm
memorare		novissima

Over the coffin Miserere mei deus, and below it Disce mori quia morieris.

Lower down in the window

The dey of Jugment.

Christ in judgment on the world; his right hand in blessing, his left stretched forth. An angel bearing the lance and sponge, other angels sounding trumpets. The right side of the piece much shattered, but still the two words patris mei of the decree of benediction. On the left a man standing, and above him a scroll with the sentence of everlasting doom Ito maledictu' i' igne' eternu'. Many bodies rising from tombs, some with only the head appearing, others half out. Both pieces simply sketched and tinted in yellow.

All the floors in the Church are modern, being flagged or bricked, and are raised considerably above the old ones. In making new the floor of the South Aisle in 1809 some encaustic tiles were brought to light. Part of them was sold and went to adorn the entrance hall of a gentleman's house in the town, four-hundred were placed in the Chancel within the Communion rails. They are charged with various devices and arms, the ground being red and the figures yellow. Amongst them a fess between 6 cross-croslets [Beauchamp, Earl of Warwick] : 3 chevronells : a lion passant-guardant, fleur-de-liz, and letter 𝕸. In the soil of the Crypt floor fragments of glazed tiles red and black have been found over a layer of mortar, all which show what the old pavement was, and its level too.

Only twelve monuments and tombstones in the Church are known as going back to the time when it was collegiate, and it is a matter of historical research to find out whom each of them except one has pourtrayed in stone, or brass, or black outline.

In the N. wall of St. George's Chapel under a simple-pointed arch is a recumbent figure in freestone close to the floor, the head resting on a pillow, the feet on a dog, and the hands joined in prayer. The whole is much broken and decayed, and the face has been chiselled away. But the costume is that of a secular canon, which consisted of a cassock, a surplice, and the *almutium* or tippet with long lappets in front and a hood here drawn over the head. Is not this the tomb of Baldwin de Whitney, Dean of Tamworth who died in 1369 ? It seems to be. For this monument of a dignitary of a chapter is coeval with the Chapel built here first after the Church was burnt down in 1345. Now this Baldwin was the only Dean between that year and 1400 who died possessed of his benefice at Tamworth. As a friend of Sir Baldwin de Frevile he appears in some Castle deeds, so that he must have dwelt here. And at that period none of the Canons were in residence who died still holding their Prebends in this Church. Hence this lowly monument may be looked on with a deep and a double interest, not only as showing the dress of the Canons here, but also as the memorial of the Dean who was probably the founder of this Chapel, and under whose charge the Church was built again on a scale and in a style remarkable alike for excellence and beauty.

Under a similar pointed arch below the window of the North Transept is the recumbent figure of a warrior arrayed in chain-mail, with the surcoat over the haubert, and the sword-belt, the head seemingly on a helmet and the hands once in prayer on the breast. But the whole has been much worn by time and so mutilated in the Civil Wars that the hands and arms and the lower portions of the figure are gone except part of a leg and a foot. A neat mural tablet erected close by in 1725 records this as a monument of the extinct family of Comberford, and mentions the building of the Comberford-Chapel. " Hic situm est Monumentum, diuternitate vero temporis et bellis plusquam civilibus dirutum, familiæ non ita pridem florentis gentis, ampliæ et honestæ Comberfordiorum, qui de hoc municipio cum in aliis tum in hoc Templo ædificando optime meruerunt." We may suppose this to be the tomb of the founder of the Chapel, and to represent either William de Comberford who is last mentioned in 1349, or (if it was erected during life as was often the case) his son John who died about the end of the same century. In 1809 this monument was hidden when the great stairs into the gallery of the Aisle were built.

Under the second arch between the Choir and Chantry-Chapel a large altar-tomb of freestone and on it the full-sized figure of a female, her head on a pillow and her feet on a dog: the arms broken off and every feature of the face and mark of the dress worn away. At each corner of the tomb three little buttresses and along each side six decorated compartments each with a shield plain or defaced. The ends of the tomb hidden against the sides of the arch. The whole is in the style of the middle of the 14th century, and we believe that this is the monument of Lady Jane de Frevile who died about the beginning of October 1339. It was perfect when Dugdale gave an engraving of it.

Under the third arch between the Choir and Chantry-Chapel a large altar-tomb of freestone, with small plain shields on the sides alternating with a rose, an oak-leaf, or some other flower.

On the slab a knight in armour, his head on a helmet and feet on a dog, and his wife to his left side. The arms of both figures and the legs of the man from the hips to the ankles are gone and almost all the details of costume worn away. Dugdale has an engraving of it whole. We believe this to be the tomb of Sir Baldwin Frevile 14th lord of the Castle and of Jane his wife daughter of Sir Thomas Green knt.: he died at Middleton Hall Oct. 4th 1400 in the 32nd year of his age, being the fourth in his family of those who bore the same Christian name and held the Castle. Our reasons for giving the monument to him seem to be strong. We have already quoted Leland as to the fair tombs here, " where of one," says he in a varied reading of his MSS., " is of the Frevills, and his Christen Name, as some say, was Balduinus; and he was Lorde of Tamworthe Castle." Now, of the five Baldwins the first died abroad, the second had two wives, the widow of the third was married again and lived away from Tamworth, and the fifth died in his nonage and single, after whom the Castle passed by his sister into the family of Ferrers. Architectural details bear us out in our point.

In the Choir by the side of Lady Jane de Frevile's monument an altar-tomb of freestone with ornamented compartments on the sides; in each compartment an angel supporting before him a shield plain or defaced. On the top a slab of

Derbyshire marble once inlaid with brass having the outlines of a knight in armour with his sword on his side, and of a lady on his left, the head of each resting on a separate cushion. Under him the marks for seven children, under her for about as many more. The principal figures beneath a double canopy, and near each corner of the stone the mark of an escutcheon. Along the bevelled margin of the slab a groove for an inscription. Here Sir Thomas Ferrers, knt., must have been interred, who died August 22nd 1498 when he was about 76 years old. By his will dated Feb. 10th 1496-7 he ordered his body to be buried on the N. side of the Choir by the side of his wife (Ann daughter of Sir Leonard Hastings, knt., of Kirby in Leicestersh.) and directed a marble to be laid over them with their portraitures and arms in brass and such inscription as his executors should devise. When Leland wrote of Tamworth Sir Humfrey Ferrers owned the Castle, whose grandfather and grandmother he says lay here. He erred if he had only this tomb in view, for Sir Thomas was great-grandfather to Sir Humfrey. The grandfather Sir John Ferrers, knt., died in his father's lifetime about 1485, and his widow Matilda or Maud (daughter of Sir John Stanley, knt., of Elford) being married again to John Agard, Esq., of Tutbury and still alive with him in 1506 would in all likelihood be buried with her second husband or his family.

Under the first arch between the Choir and Chantry-Chapel a fine altar-tomb of Derbyshire marble once painted and matched with coloured decorations of the arch, to the memory of Sir John Ferrers, knt., who died July 16th 1512 aged 44 years, and of Lady Dorothy his wife. By his will he ordered his body to be buried in the Choir before the Image of St. Edith. This tomb seems to stand where it was first placed, but the front slab has been turned round into its present position from facing the Choir, and this must have been done when the large modern monument of the Ferrers family dated in the year 1680 was placed against the S. side of the arch. It bears the figures of a knight and his lady on his left side both recumbent in prayer. The knight in armour with his sword on his side, wearing the SS collar, his uncovered head on a helmet and feet on a dog. The lady's head on a cushion and at her feet a little dog crouching and holding her dress in its mouth. By the cushion the figure of an infant. One side and both ends of the tomb hidden in the masonry around; along the exposed side twelve canopied niches with figures standing in prayer, but the 5th and 11th now gone. The faces, hands, and other parts of the chief figures and heads and hands of the smaller ones on the side have been chiselled away. Running along the upper margin of the front the following inscription is cut in raised characters:

𝔥𝔦𝔠 𝔧𝔞𝔠𝔢𝔫𝔱 𝔠𝔬𝔯𝔭𝔬𝔯𝔞 𝔍𝔬𝔥'𝔦𝔰 𝔉𝔢𝔯𝔯𝔢𝔯𝔰 𝔪𝔦𝔩𝔦𝔱𝔦𝔰 𝔢𝔱 𝔡'𝔫𝔢 𝔇𝔬𝔯𝔬𝔱𝔥𝔢𝔢 𝔟𝔯𝔬𝔯𝔦𝔰 𝔢𝔦𝔲𝔰 𝔮𝔲𝔦 𝔮𝔲𝔦𝔡' 𝔍𝔬𝔥'𝔢𝔰 𝔬𝔟𝔦𝔦𝔱 𝔵𝔟𝔧 𝔡𝔦𝔢 𝔪𝔢𝔫𝔰𝔦𝔰 𝔧𝔲𝔩𝔦𝔦 𝔄𝔫𝔫𝔬 𝔡'𝔫𝔦 𝔪ᵒ𝔡ᵒ𝔵𝔦𝔦 𝔢𝔱 𝔡𝔦𝔠𝔱𝔞 𝔡'𝔫𝔞 𝔇𝔬𝔯𝔬𝔱𝔥𝔢𝔞 𝔬𝔟𝔦𝔦𝔱   𝔡𝔦𝔢 𝔪𝔢'𝔰   𝔞𝔫𝔫𝔬 𝔡'𝔫𝔦 𝔐ᵒ𝔡ᵒ   𝔔𝔲𝔬𝔯' 𝔞𝔦'𝔞𝔟𝔲𝔰 𝔭𝔯𝔬𝔭𝔦𝔠𝔦𝔢𝔱' 𝔡𝔢𝔲𝔰 𝔄𝔪𝔢𝔫. The date of Lady Dorothy Ferrers's death in 1532 has not been filled in.

In the middle of the Choir in the floor a large tombstone once inlaid with brass. The outlines of a priest with a label from his mouth, of a chalice on each side and below him, of an escutcheon at each corner, and of a marginal inscription with circles at the corners as if for the emblems of the four Evangelists. Here must be grave of Master Humfrey Wystowe, Dean, who died in 1514.

In the floor of the Chantry-Chapel close to the monument in the N. wall a large alabaster tombstone once with figures and a marginal inscription cut in and filled with pitch, but almost wholly worn away. In 1840 we could just decipher,

………𝔠𝔢𝔫𝔱 𝔠𝔬𝔯𝔭𝔬𝔯𝔞…………………………

………𝔬𝔫 𝔤𝔢𝔫𝔢𝔯𝔬𝔰𝔦 𝔢𝔱……𝔲…………𝔢………………

……………………………………………………………………

………………𝔬𝔟𝔦𝔦𝔱 𝔟𝔦𝔦 𝔡𝔦𝔢…………………

To the left adjoining, a stone once inlaid with brass with the outline of a man, his sword at his left side. Near the upper corners marks for two escutcheons and near the lower ones two circles. A groove for a marginal inscription.

Again to the left adjoining an alabaster stone
and on it cut in black outline the figure of a
man praying, his head on a pillow and a scrip at
his right side. The worn-out parts of the inscription are given by Thomas and Shaw. We copied
it in 1840; twelve years later all was obliterated.

✠ 𝕺rate pro anima 𝕵oh'is [Breton filii & heredis
Ric. Breton de Tamworth armigeri] qui
obiit xi die mens' maii anno d'ni m°d°bii:
cuius a'i'e p'picietur deus.

A little beyond the last but one, a large flat
stone with marks for brass plates. A man praying, his feet on a dog. From his mouth a label,
on each side of him six small scrolls and one
under him. A groove for a marginal inscription,
with circles cut out at the corners.

Thomas and (more correctly) Shaw give an
inscription in black-letter for one of these unknown stones.

Hic jacet Wylelmus Repyngton de
Amyngtone armiger et Julyana uxor qui
obiit xxx die Januarii Anno M.D. xxxxiii.
cujus anime propicietur Deus. Amen.

At the W. end of the South Aisle in the floor a
stone with the marks of brasses for a man, an
escutcheon above him, on each side of it a child,
in the corners four squares, and around the whole
a groove for an inscription in the margin.

SEAL. We have seen only one impression of
the common seal of the Church used before the

Common Seal.

(Time of Henry VIII.)

THE RESTORATION OF TAMWORTH PARISH CHURCH.

THE work of Restoration of the interior of the Church being now completed in accordance with the several contracts, the Committee, in discharge of the duties undertaken by them, proceed to lay before their fellow Parishioners the following Report :—

Statement of Accounts.

Messrs. Wood, for the general Repairs, New Seats, &c....	2874	1	3
Mr. Edwards, for the Heating Apparatus	325	0	0
Mr. Holdich, Improving and Rebuilding the Organ	268	0	0
Mr. Butterfield, Architect...	191	1	6
Messrs. Chinn, Lichfield, for Faculty ...	18	3	2
Removing Bones from Crypt and interring them	11	5	0
Advertisements	3	3	0
Sundry small Accounts	20	0	0
	£3710	**13**	**11**

Of this amount some part is still outstanding ; but when the promised Grant of £190 from the Diocesan Society is received, the Committee will be in a position to pay off the balance with the exception of about £60, of which they will be deficient.

The Committee feel justified in congratulating their fellow-Parishioners on the amount of work which has been done, and on the very great improvement that has been effected in the appearance and also in the comfort and general convenience of their Parish Church, at a comparatively moderate expense.

But although much has been done,— and, in addition to the contract works, some important parts of the Restoration have been effected by special Donations.—the Committee are aware that much still remains to be done ; and it becomes their duty to lay before the Parishioners a statement of such additional reparations as are required to complete the interior.

These, taken in their natural order of precedence, appear to be as follows :—

1.—Gas Fittings for Lighting the Church.

2. - A new Enclosure to the Western Entrance.

3.—To repair and re-arrange the Steps and Paved Ways of the Church Yard.

4.—To restore the Clerestory Windows on the North Side of the Nave, which are in an unsafe state.

5.—To restore the Pillars of the Nave, and the Stonework of the West Door, and to put a new Door.

6.—To scrape and restore the face of the Clerestory Walls.

7.—To restore the Piers at the entrance of the Chancel.

8.—To complete the Restoration of the large Norman Arches.

9.—To repair the Monumental Arches in the Chancel and the Jambs of the Windows over them.

10.—To complete the Restoration of the Arches, Responds, and Walls of the North and South Transepts.

For these and other desirable Works about £800 will probably be required.

The Committee propose to lay this Report more formally before a Meeting of the Parishioners, with the hope that a new effort will be made to raise the above sum by a general Subscription.

Sep. 18, 1871.

year 1500, and that was much broken. It was oval, and seemed to have had in the centre the figure of St. Edith, and inscribed around,

......Ium commune ec...............................

Thomas Parker, Dean from 1525 to 1538, had a seal made up for this Church by changing the lettering and arms in a fine large oval seal which had been made after the reign of Henry IV. for some other foundation. We give an engraving of this seal. Five canopied figures: the B. Virgin and Child, an archbishop, a bishop, St. Katherine with wheel and sword, a bishop praying. The debased lettering out of character with the rest: S·COMVNE·COLLEGIATE·DE·ToWORTH. On one escutcheon where may still be traced the original arms in the three fleurs-de-liz of the 1st and 4th quarterings of England and France, the initials T P. On the other escutcheon the arms of Parker. The brass matrix of this seal in the possession of William Staunton, Esq., of Longbridge House near Warwick.

NOTE.

We have described the fabric of the old Collegiate Church as far as the details were to be gathered twenty years ago. Since that time and more particularly within the last two years great alterations and restorations have changed the aspect of the whole interior of the building. The alterations of 1869 and 1870 may be thus summed up. ✳

In the Chancel (Choir) the large E. window reconstructed and filled with stained glass as a testimonial from the Parishioners and others to the late Vicar, Rev. Dr. Millar, now Vicar of Cirencester; the Norman window into the South Chancel (South Transept) and the three windows into the North Chancel (Chantry Chapel) opened again; the altar-tomb of Lady Jane Frevile renovated by Francis Willington, Esq., of Tamworth, who justly claims her as his ancestress; and the altar-tomb of Sir Thomas Ferrers altogether taken away. The W. piers of the two Norman arches pierced with apertures at some height from the ground, giving a view of the Chancel from the Aisles. The floor of the North Transept and North Chancel raised to the level of the rest of the Church, and the high pews within the Norman arches removed, so as to allow sittings in the North and South Chancels. The brickt-up arches between the Aisles and North and South Chancels opened, and the staircases into the galleries removed, on the N. side bringing the Comberford monument to light again. The old font which long stood in the South Chancel renovated and placed under the North Norman arch. A window in the South Chancel handsomely filled with stained glass to the memory of John Harding, Esq., formerly of Bonehill, by his daughter Miss Harding of Tamworth. The whole S. wall of the two Sacristies rebuilt. The larger Sacristy changed into the Clergy Vestry, with only the door into the Chancel, and a new one from the outer Sacristy, and an E. and a S. window. The smaller Sacristy now cut off from the Chancel, and divided into two by a low screen-wall with a door, thus forming an outer Sacristy and a new public entrance by a S. door with a window above, each part of this late Vestry being also entered by a door from the South Chancel. ✝ In the Nave the organ and organ-gallery at the W. end removed, the organ being placed in the S. Chancel between the two new door-ways and against the E. wall on which the ancient paintings were; the window between the Nave and Tower reopened and filled with sheets of glass. ✝ The doorway in the South Aisle, where the Porch had been, opened again and restored according to the old details. The pews on the ground-floor replaced by open seats, and portions of the N. and S. galleries in the Aisles removed.

The Crypt emptied of the bones which in Nov. 1869 were buried in the N.E. corner of the Churchyard, a part of the Crypt being partitioned off to lodge the heating apparatus of the building, the old doorway closed, and an entrance formed from the outside, with a descent of twelve steps and a pointed doorway made on a level with the Crypt floor. Every one of the old tombstones in the floor of the Church have disappeared, so that out of the twelve we have detailed only five remain, which are those with effigies.

The E. end of the Chancel is now decorated with a fine Reredos carved in stone, which was put up in 1852.

Such have been the latest changes in the buildings. We have recorded them (although it has not been within the scope of our present work to note all the alterations made within the last three centuries) because, whilst obliterating many a debased architectural detail which modern taste and convenience had brought in, they have also materially modified several great features of the ancient structure. The time will come when only the pen of the historian will distinguish between what is original and what is skilful copy. The total expense of the last alterations has been about 3830*l.*

Churchyard.

The ancient Churchyard measured about three-fourths of the present one in breadth. It was enclosed all around with stone walls. There were two or three entrances and one of them was by a stile facing Cokets Lane. The land next this stile given by Milisand atte Castel for restoring the Church had been granted to Adam de Castro and to her by the Bailiffs, Burgesses and Commonalty of the Town May 4th 1340 to be held by service of 6d. a year for ever, and it was 24 ft.

long and $7\frac{1}{2}$ ft. broad. On this plot and over a
Lych-gate some chambers were afterwards built
for the abode of a chaplain, which at last were
made into two small dwellings. The Lych-gate
was removed early in the last century.

In the Great Courts of the Staffordshire side of
the town many bye-laws were made for keeping
the Churchyard in order. Oct. 8th 1409: as
Rich. Dalton and his tenants have put guts and
garbage of beasts outside his house to the nuisance of those going into the Churchyard he shall
amend it by next All Saints' day, under pain of
40d. to the Commonalty and 40d. to the Bailiffs.
Oct. 21st 1421: no one to put any animal into the
Churchyard violating it, under pain of 40d. half
to the Church and half to the common box (of
the town). May 1st 1425 and Nov. 24th 1427:
no one to winnow grain in the Churchyard, under
pain of 20d. half to the Bailiffs and half to the
common box. Oct. 18th 1435: no one to winnow
corn in the Churchyard, under pain of 12d. July
10th 1436: no butcher to throw dung under the
Church wall, "& in p'bendr' de Coton," under
pain of 20d. half to the common box and the rest
to the Bailiffs. Nov. 3rd 1444: no one to put
muck on the Church stile, under pain of 12d.
half to the Bailiffs and half to the common box.
May 1st 1453: no one to put muck under the
Church wall, under pain of 6s. 8d. to be shared
as the last. Oct. 21st 1511: no inhabitants to

let pigs go at large within the town or in the Churchyard, under pain of 4*d*. for each pig, half to the catcher and half to the common box. Apr. — 1517 : those who have pigs to keep them out of the Market Place and Churchyard, under pain of 1*d*. a pig, half to the Church and half to the Chamberlains (of the town). May 2nd 1519 : no one hereafter to put his horse or horses into the Churchyard, under pain of 14*d*. each time to the *prefect* [Dean or his Vicar] of the Church. Oct. 18th 1546 : no one to play in places forbidden by the statutes of the realm and above all in the Churchyard, under pain of 6*s*. 8*d*. each time ; nor to winnow grain or corn there to the grievous nuisance of the Church, under the like pain.

At the Court held July 10th 1436 Tho. de Coton was amerced 12*d*. for carrying off some wheat in the Churchyard, and William Newport, Dean, 12*d*. for winnowing wheat ; and Oct. 21st 1505 Rich. Alcoke 4*d*. for *wenoyng chayfe* there. Amercements are continually on record for nuisances under the Churchyard wall in Church Street, and within the Churchyard.

There is not one ancient tombstone left.

Dean's House.

Between the E. side of the Churchyard and Gungate stand two low parallel walls built of ragstone with tiles inserted, all in the English style before the Conquest. These walls now serve only as boundaries to yards and gardens, and support sties and sheds. In the N. wall are some traces of a window and half a fireplace and chimney. These ruins are all that is now left of the ancient Dean's house. Another wall with two semi-circular arches in it once joined the present walls, but it was pulled down in 1797 when the E. boundary wall of the Churchyard was built. Between the walls is now a garden, and in it was once some cellaring, where romping children felt their hearts beat quick when winds went whistling through the gloomy vaults and scared them from the haunted steps. About the end of last century the roofs sank and the cellars were filled up with soil. The Dean's house reached to Little College Lane on the N., and the Deanery Gate was in Gungate, but there was always a row of houses between this mansion and Church Street. This dwelling-house of the Deans was burnt down on Thursday June 15th 1559 in a fire which destroyed Bolebridge Street, Colehill, and parts of George Street, Church Street and Gungate, and was kept within bounds only by crofts, gardens, and void lands in various parts of the town.

To the N.W. of Ellergate (now Aldergate) lay the Dean's Croft, with the Dean's Pool, and the Dean's Barn or Tithe Barn, which are often spoken of in the records of the town before the middle of the sixteenth century. All are gone long ago. The notices of the Pool, however, seem exactly to point to one which in our early days was surrounded with tall poplars in a large field. The trees have disappeared and the plough now passes over the pool. It was here that a lovelorn young woman drowned herself about sixty years ago; and a soldier had to prove to the common people his guiltlessness of her murder, by publicly touching the corpse, which did not bleed nor shrink whilst he knelt and went through the painful ceremony. A doleful ballad on the subject was once popular in the town and neighbourhood, but is now quite forgotten.

Stone Cross.

The Stone Cross stood near the Dean's House in the open space where Church Street, Colehill, and Gungate meet, and just within the Staffordshire side of the town. It is mentioned early in the reign of Edward I. At the Great Court held Oct. 18th 1516 it was ordered that butchers should no more sharpen their axes or knives on the Cross, under pain of 12*d.* for each to the (common) box. On new year's day (Mar. 25th) a prescriptive fair was held here for the Staffordshire side, but it dwindled away after the government of the town was vested in one Corporate Body three centuries ago.

The Cross has been long destroyed. The stones of the round steps were set up to form the horse-block of an inn and to mark out the Pig Market close by. Even these worn-out relics disappeared in Sept. 1852, and now the only memorial of this ancient monument on the spot is the sign of the inn "The Old Stone Cross."

CHAPTER VII.

FASTI ECCLESIÆ, OR CALENDAR OF THE DIGNITARIES OF THE CHURCH, &c.

OUR notices of institutions or admissions to the Prebends taken from the Episcopal Registers of Lichfield down to the year 1400 are due to the hired researches of a stranger. We have no reasons to distrust what he has gathered, though we believe that there must be several omissions. We can answer for the correctness of the rest.

1. DEANS.

MATTHEW was Dean of Tamworth in 1257 when the Chapter bought the Church of Middleton.

RALPH DE MANTON clerk was presented by Sir Philip Marmion in the time of Edward I.

JOHN DE TEFORD or THEFORD clerk was also presented by Sir Philip Marmion and appears in 1292. He resigned.

ROGER LE WYNE clerk presented by Lady Jane Morteyn died in 1305.

WALTER DE BEDEWYNDE clerk being presented by Alexander de Frevile and Jane his wife was admitted Oct. 24th 1305 and gave up in 1310.

HUGH DE BABYNGTON clerk also presented by Alexander and Jane was admitted Nov. 15th 1310. Some cause or other in the Bishop's Court made him resign at the close of 1312; but he appealed to the Archbishop of Canterbury, and an inhibition prevented the bishop from acting anywise against him. Thus he continued in the office of Dean, and as such appears in a plea of debt in 1313 against John le Blound of Lichfield chaplain, in the Courts of the Staffordshire side of the town. In Trinity term 1315 Jane late wife of Thomas de Lodelow (her husband had died in the Spring of 1314) carried her claim to present in due turn into the Court of Common Pleas. On her behalf it was alleged that Alexander and Jane had presented Bedewynde as heirs of Mazera le Crumwell and that in the case of Babyngton they had taken the turn falling to Ralph le Botiller. Ralph le Botiller freely allowed the claim, saving his own right; Alexander and Jane answered merely that there was no vacancy. But the bishop's certificate being thereon required went to show that the Deanery had been vacant from Sunday in the feast of St. Silvester (Dec. 31st) 1312. In the mean time however a private agreement was made in favour of the claimant, for whom judgment in her plea followed in Hillary term 1316-7, and she had as damages the moiety of the yearly value of the Deanery instead of 100*l.* at which they had been laid.

HENRY DE CLYFF being thus presented by Jane late wife of Tho. de Lodelow was instituted Jan. 16th 1316-7. He had royal letters of protection June 8th following and July 30th 1318, each time for one year.

ISAMBERT DE LONGA VILLA physician probably to Edward II., being over-sea in the royal service with the king, also had letters of protection June 5th 1320 to last till the Assumption. He died in 1328 or 1329.

RICHARD DE GLOUCESTRE clerk had the king's letters of presentation June 22nd 1328, the Deanery being void (it was said) and in the gift of the crown, as the lands etc. of Alex. de Frevile deceased who held them *in capite* were in the king's hands. We doubt whether he took the Deanery.

ROBERT CIONI DE CHERCALDO clerk had the king's gift Aug. 22nd 1329 to this Deanery which Master Isambert *medicus* now dead lately had. Against any royal appointment Lady Jane de Frevile petitioned the king and his council. Her husband Sir Alex. de Frevile she said held the Castle in her right, and by royal licence it had been settled on herself after his death and on her son Baldwin after her; and the advowson of the Deanery and Prebends pertained to the Castle. This was all true we find as to the Castle according to the inquisition of Dec. 19th and the licence of Dec. 30th 1323 and the fine levied in the king's court at the next Easter, but throughout nothing was said as to the Church.

BALDWIN DE WHITNEY clerk was admitted Feb. 22nd 1329-30. He had royal ratification as Dean Jan. 23rd 1347-8 and died in 1369.

WALTER PRYDE chaplain was presented by the king Aug. 23rd 1369 and instituted Sept. 2nd following.

From this time all the presentations to the Deanery were made by the king.

REGINALD DE HULTON or HILTON clerk exchanged with the last his Parsonage of Holsworthy in the diocese of Exeter for this Deanery, to which Aug. 3rd 1372 he had the royal presentation. After seventeen years he again exchanged for a Prebend of the Church of St. Mary in Leicester Castle with the next.

THOMAS IBERYE clerk had the king's letters Dec. 3rd 1389, and on the 16th was admitted to the Deanery.

WILLIAM COTYNGHAM clerk was presented Sept. 20th 1390·

JOHN DE MASSYNGHAM clerk parson of Agmondesham exchanged with Iberye, and was presented May 1st 1391. According to the Bishop's Register he was admitted June 28th after Cotyngham.

JOHN BERNARD clerk parson of Hatfield Episcopi exchanged that living with Massyngham, and Dec. 18th 1399 had the Deanery given to him.

WILLIAM POUNTFREYT clerk was presented Feb. 10th 1403-4, but does not appear to have taken the Deanery.

CLEMENT DENSTON had the royal gift Feb. 15th 1428-9, having exchanged with Bernard for the Prebend of Keton in St. Martin le Grand, London.

THOMAS RODEBOURNE exchanged the Archdeaconry of Sudbury with Denston, and Apr. 18th 1429 received the Deanery. He gave up on being raised to the Bishopric of St. David's, and died about 1442.

JOHN DELABERE clerk late Grand Almoner to the king was presented Feb. 1st 1432-3, but soon exchanged with his successor here for a Canonry in Exeter Cathedral. In 1447 he became bishop of St. David's, and surrendered his See about the end of 1460, being then very old.

WILLIAM NEWPORT was presented May 13th 1434, and died about two years after.

JOHN BATE clerk had the Deanery given him Aug. 26th 1436, and at the same time a mandate was directed to the Bailiffs of the town and to Robert Bate to put him into possession. He received the king's ratification Nov. 3rd 1461. He was a clerk then a Master in Chancery, and had a royal pardon in the usual form Feb. 13th 1467-8 which the troubles of those times required. He died in 1479.

RALPH FERRERS clerk a younger son of Sir Thomas Ferrers was presented July 27th 1479, and ceased by death in 1504.

THOMAS BOWDE clerk followed Sept. 28th 1504.

WILLIAM LICHFIELD clerk gave up the Deanery in 1512 when his successor was appointed.

HUMFREY WYSTOWE S.T.P. was presented Dec. 12th 1512. He probably belonged to an honourable family of his surname in Tamworth where he dwelt whilst he was beneficed here. He was a Fellow of All Souls College, Oxford, in 1499 was Principal of St. Edmund's Hall, and June 19th 1509 took the degree of D.D. Dying in Oct. 1514 he was buried in the Choir of this Church.

WILLIAM HONE clerk was presented Oct. 28th 1514, and died about 1522.

RICHARD RAWSON clerk succeeded Apr. 10th 1522; he made

an exchange with the next for the Rectory of Bekingsfield in the Diocese of Lincoln.

THOMAS PARKER B. Dec. had the Deanery May 27th 1525. The next year he was also made Dean of Stafford, and had then graduated as Doctor. From 1522 to 1535 he was Chancellor of Worcester, afterwards of Salisbury till his death in Aug. 1538. He was brother to the Abbot of Gloucester. When he died, Cranmer, Archbishop of Canterbury, wrote (Aug. 28th) to the Vicar-General Crumwell, praising up Dr. Barons (probably Dr. Barnes who within two years after suffered death for his religious opinions) for this Deanery, as Staffordshire was destitute of learned men and preachers: meaning thereby such as went in for the King's Supremacy. But the recommendation did not avail.

SIMON SYMONDS clerk was presented Oct. 17th 1538, and was the last Dean of Tamworth. He died in 1551 a Canon of Windsor.

2. PREBENDARIES OF SYERSCOTE.

ADAM DE WALTONE is named in 1292.

RICHARD DE TECCEBURY was admitted Oct. 12th 1303 on the presentation of Tho. de Lodelow and Jane his wife, and was living in 1318.

ROBERT DE FREFORD.

JOHN DE GREY clk. was presented by the king Apr. 29th 1348.

HUGH DE HOPEWAS nevertheless exchanged the Church of Davenham for this Prebend with Freford, was presented Mar. 8th 1348-9 by the king on account of the lands etc. of Henry Hillary deceased being in the royal hands, and was admitted May 1st following. He belonged to that younger but still wealthy off-shoot of the Hopewas family which was settled at Tamworth. One after the other he held the Rectory of Barwell in Leicestersh. and the Church of Clifton Campville in Staffordsh., being admitted to the former Dec. 27th 1349 on the presentation of the Abbess and Convent of Polesworth, and to the latter Aug. 8th 1353 on that of Sir Rich. de Stafford. On June 13th 1360 he had the king's mortmain licence to give 100s. a-year in land and rent for a chaplain to celebrate at Clifton Campville and thus founded a Chantry there for the ghostly welfare of Sir Rich. de Stafford his patron and Sir Richard's wife Maud and former wife Isabel. He was appointed Chancellor or Vicar-General of the Diocese in 1358, exchanged the Prebend of Syerscote for that of Curborough in Lichfield Cathedral May 20th 1363, and died in 1382.

From 1363 the presentations to the Prebends belonged wholly to the Crown.

JOHN DE DEPYNG had royal letters for this Prebend dated Dec. 10th 1363, but gave it up within three years.

RALPH GENTIL was presented Oct. 14th and admitted Nov. 2nd 1366. He exchanged for the Church of West Kirkby in the Diocese of Coventry and Lichfield with the next.

SIMON GENTIL clerk was presented Feb. 12th 1367-8.

JOHN EDWARD clerk was presented Aug. 15th and admitted on the 25th 1369. He died in 1383.

JOHN DE WODEHOUS clerk king's chamberlain of N. Wales and Chester was presented Nov. 24th and admitted Dec. 1st 1383 and continued till his death in 1395.

GUY MONE or MOONE clerk was presented Nov. 2nd and admitted on the 20th 1395.

NICHOLAS SLAKE clerk had been presented Aug. 15th before Mone, who gave up: Slake was again presented Jan. 10th and had institution Feb. 24th 1395-6.

RALPH CANON chaplain of the Wolseley Chantry in the Church of Colwich exchanged with Slake and had this Prebend given him Nov. 16th 1399.

THOMAS SHELFORD clerk was presented Dec. 2nd 1405.

THOMAS SHEPEY came next, whose death it seems was wrongly reported in 1456.

JOHN ARUNDEL clerk first physician to King Henry VI. received the royal gift Feb. 16th 1456-7.

THOMAS HAWEKYNS clerk was however presented May 21st 1460, on the resignation of Thomas *Schippey*.

ROBERT SLYMBRIGGE clerk succeeded June 4th 1463 and followed the example of his predecessor in quickly resigning.

THOMAS BALSALLE clerk, of Merton College, and Procter of the University in 1451, was presented Jan. 14th 1464-5.

WILLIAM SMYTH clerk resigned in 1504.

HUMFREY WYSTOWE clerk was presented Apr. 1st 1504, and continued till he became Dean.

JOHN LICHEFELD clerk succeeded Dec. 12th 1512.

THOMAS LOWE was presented Mar. 30th 1523.

JOHN FYSHER clerk was the last Prebendary of Syerscote.

3. PREBENDARIES OF WILNECOTE.

In the course of our latest researches we accidentally met with some documents in the Public Record Office, which chiefly concern the Prebend of Wilnecote. We embody all this fresh matter here, first of all noting three points in what we have already given.

1st. The yearly service of half a mark rendered to the Church of Tamworth for the Manor of Middleton (*see p.* 15) was paid with great solemnity at the High Altar on the feast of St. Edith.

2nd. Lady Mary Marmion died about midsummer 1313 (*see p.* 19), for the earliest writ to an escheator to enquire into what she had held *in capite* was issued July 16th in that year. The writ and inquisition for Tamworth dated respectively Nov. 1st and Dec. 18th 1314 must have been notably delayed.

3rd. Ralph le Botiller junior was not childless (*see p.* 18), for the *consanguineus* by whom he was succeeded was not a *cousin* as is generally stated, but a grandson (*kinsman*) named Ralph, who was a minor and became a ward of the Crown. This Ralph le Botiller junior outlived his son John and died when he was sixty years old. John was father of Ralph the minor and closed his life at *Coloyne* Aug. 29th 1337, when Edward his younger son (born and baptized at *Hattele* co. Beds. July 20th) was six weeks old. Edward was brother and at last heir of Ralph le Botiller the minor.

HUGH DE CAVE clerk was presented by Sir Philip Marmion, and died in 1298.

SIMON DE WYCFORD clerk belonged to a family that held much real property in Tamworth, and he was married before he entered Holy Orders. He was admitted to this Prebend in 1298 [1299 ?] after the death of Cave, being presented by Sir Ralph Basset of Drayton, son of that Sir Ralph to whom and to whose heirs Lady Mary Marmion demised her Prebends here. At her death this Prebend was valued at 4*l.* instead of 5*l.* In the partition of her estates made at Middleton June 19th 1315, nothing was said as to this Church. Matilda daughter of Sir Philip Marmion died between 1292 and 1295, and her husband Ralph le Botiller senior in the spring of 1307. Their son Ralph junior claimed his inheritance of the two Prebends which were taken into the king's hands at Lady Mary's decease. On Apr. 17th 1317 a royal mandate was issued for Alexander and Jane de Frevile and Jane widow of Thomas de Lodelow to appear in the Court of Chancery May 16th and receive their pourparty of the advowsons: on the 28th this Prebend was assigned to Ralph le Botiller junior and the escheator was commanded to deliver it to him. When Simon de Wycford died, Lady Jane de Frevile, Ralph le Botiller junior and Henry and Jane Hillary contended for the presentation; but by a private composition dated at Sutton Coldfield Aug. 14th 1334 it was agreed that Lady Jane de Frevile as eldest should exercise the right in this first vacancy, Ralph in the second, and Henry and Jane in the third, and so on and for their heirs. This agreement did not hinder Lady Jane de Frevile in petitioning in Chancery for her pourparty of the advowsons. On Sept. 24th 1337 it was directed that she should be heard in the three weeks of Michaelmas, and the escheator was to make this known to Botiller and the Hillaries. But the writ was not delivered to the escheator till Oct. 12th too late for execution.

THOMAS DE BLASTON being presented by Lady Jane de Frevile was admitted Aug. 15th 1334. He died in 1342.

THOMAS DE WHITNEY was presented by Baldwin de Frevile, and was instituted Sept. 3rd 1342. But this right to take the turn falling by the composition of 1334 to Ralph le Botiller the minor was challenged by the king, who claimed the gift on account of the wardship and issued a writ of *Quare impedit* against the Lord of the Castle. The arguments on the question were long, learned, and full of law, so as to form afterwards a standing precedent in cases of the same kind. The upshot of the matter was that the right of the crown was established.

JOHN DE KYNEWELL, GYNEWELL, GYNDWELL, or CYNEWELL clerk who had been presented by the king Sept. 10th 1342, "r'one custodie t're & h'edis Rad'i le Botiller defuncti qui de R. tenuit in capite," was admitted July 18th in the following year. He was also a Canon of Salisbury, and Mar. 23rd 1346-7 Pope Clement VI. appointed him Bishop of Lincoln: he was consecrated Sept. 23rd following, and dying Aug. 5th 1362 was buried in his own cathedral. On his being raised to the See, this Prebend became void, and Sir Henry Hillary made his presentation in the third vacancy according to the composition. But another *Quare impedit* on the part of the crown carried the matter into the court of the king's bench (damages being laid at 1000*l.*) in Michaelmas term 1347, when the royal gift of the Prebend in 1317 to Ralph le Botiller junior again decided the question. Sir Henry Hillary not only lost his cause, but was forced to sue for a royal pardon (*see p.* 20). On his part it was said *inter alia* that he had had a son Edward by Lady Jane, but now held this Prebend in right of Margaret daughter of Thomas de Lodelow, Lady Jane's son by her former husband.

HENRY DE INGELBY clerk was presented by the king June 4th 1347 "r'one Custodie t're & heredis Rad'i Botiller consanguinei & heredis Rad'i Botiller defuncti qui de R. tenuit in capite," and was admitted Sept. 17th following. He exchanged for a canonry in Darlington Church, Durham, with the next.

PHILIP DE WESTON clerk was presented Feb. 24th and 26th 1357-8 by the king, on account of the advowsons which were Philip Marmion's being in the king's hands. He resigned.

JOHN RONHALD clerk stepped into this Canonry Oct. 26th 1366 by royal gift.

WILLIAM PAKYNGTON clerk was presented June 13th 1389. He was treasurer of the royal household of Richard II. and died in 1390.

JOHN GAMUL clerk was presented July 26th 1390, and had royal ratification Nov. 8th 1399. He exchanged this Prebend and that of Eigne in Hereford Cathedral for the Deanery of Hastings and the Prebend of Wedmore in the same Cathedral.

GILBERT DE STONE was presented Mar. 5th 1400-1. He exchanged this Prebend for that of Tydryngton and Horningsham in the Church of Heytesbury in the diocese of Salisbury with the next.

JOHN FRANK clerk was presented Oct. 16th 1415.

THOMAS LANE exchanged the Prebend of Wanstraw in Wells Cathedral with the last. He was presented Oct. 20th 1424 and resigned in 1443.

ROBERT FABRI clerk was presented Oct. 26th 1443.

JOHN BATE the Dean took this Prebend, for which and for the Deanery the king granted him ratification Nov. 3rd 1461.

JOHN ARUNDEL one of the king's chaplains had this Prebend July 26th 1479. He was made Chancellor of Hereford in 1476, Dean of Exeter in 1483, and Bishop of Coventry and Lichfield in 1496, being consecrated Nov. 6th. He was translated to the See of Exeter in 1502, and died March 14th 1503-4.

NICHOLAS SKAYLEHORNE clerk died in 1493.

JOHN KYTE clerk succeeded by royal gift Aug. 27th 1493, and gave up in 1508.

THOMAS WELLYS clerk was presented Mar. 27th 1508.

WILLIAM WESTCOTE. On May 25th 1517 the king granted to John Veysy, Dean of Windsor; John Gifford knt., and Christofer Middelton the next presentation to a Prebend here, and their choice fell on Westcote in or before 1522.

RICHARD PYGOT a layman succeeded about 1534, whose name closes the list of the Prebendaries of Wilnecote. It is likely that he was presented by Humfrey Ferrers (afterwards knighted) and others. On July 2nd 1528 the king granted to Humfrey Ferrers Esq., Will. Repington gent., Hen. Hopwood draper, Hen. Sell merchant-tailor, and Will. Reynolds the advowson of the first Prebend falling void in this Church. Sir Humfrey Ferrers married as his first wife Margaret daughter of Tho. Pigot serjeant-at-law. Pygot compounded for first fruits Oct. 28th 1545.

4. PREBENDARIES OF COTON.

MICHAEL DE ORMESBY is mentioned from 1284 to 1301, and dwelt at Tamworth.

ROGER DE CLOUNGINFORD was presented by Sir Ralph Basset of Drayton on Lady Mary Marmion's grant to his father, and was admitted June 22nd 1301. At his decease there was a dispute between Lady Jane de Frevile and Henry Hillary and Jane his wife; but by an agreement made at Middleton Jan. 16th 1338-9 it was settled for Lady Jane de Frevile to present in this first vacancy, and in the second, fourth, and fifth; Henry Hillary and Jane in the third and sixth, and then each party was to have turn by turn. Lady Jane Hillary died in 1340.

ROBERT DE WHITNEY being therefore presented by Lady Jane de Frevile was admitted Jan. 25th 1338-9.

WALTER ALMALY clerk was presented by the king May 16th 1368, and died twenty-one years after.

RICHARD FELDE clerk was presented Sept. 9th 1389. Richard II. Apr. 5th 1399, and Henry IV. Nov. 12th following ratified his church-preferments including this Prebend. He died soon after.

ROBERT TUNSTALL clerk was presented Apr. 11th 1401.

JOHN STRAUNGE clerk succeeded on Tunstall's death, being presented Dec. 18th 1419. He ceased in 1423.

DREUX MALEFURMITY or MAUFURNEY followed July 16th 1423. He was Canon here for thirty-one years till he died.

WILLIAM MORLAND clerk was presented Jan. 13th 1454-5. He resigned.

NICHOLAS RAWDON or ROWEDON clerk had this Prebend given him Jan. 23rd 1464-5, and died in 1479.

EDMUND AUDELEY clerk had the royal gift May 13th 1479. From Archdeacon of Essex he was made Bishop of Rochester in 1480, was translated to Hereford in 1492 and to Salisbury in 1502, and died Aug. 23rd 1524. He resigned this Canonry on being first raised to a bishopric.

JOHN DUNMOWE or DYNMOWE clerk got this Prebend Sept. 21st 1480, but did not keep it many months.

WILLIAM KOKKYS or COCKYS clerk had it Feb. 28th following.

RICHARD BALDER clerk Master of the Chapel Royal of Barking followed Mar. 6th 1483-4 on the resignation of the last. He died in 1491.

EDWARD HASELEY who had been instructor in grammar to Henry VII. when a boy, was presented July 19th 1491. He became also Dean of Warwick, and died in 1506.

WALTER WOLMERE clerk had this Prebend called *Cotton Harewyke* Dec. 19th 1506. He died and his stall was taken by the next.

THOMAS HALL one of the Ministers of the Chapel Royal was presented May 8th 1522, whose decease happened in 1540.

JOHN SYNGER clerk a chaplain to the royal family had the king's presentation Aug. 8th 1540, and was the last Prebendary of Coton.

5. PREBENDARIES OF WIGGINTON AND COMBERFORD.

ROBERT DE PYCCHEFORD, PYKFORD or PYGFORD occurs in 1290. He had royal letters of protection Oct. 18th 1294 as Canon of Tamworth and parson of Hoginton and Picheford.

HENRY LE STOKE DE SOLIHULL was admitted June 18th 1311, being presented by Ralph le Botiller junior.

THOMAS LE BOTILLER was admitted May 5th 1341, and

had royal ratification Dec. 10th 1347 to this Prebend of Wigginton and Comberford.

THOMAS DE KEYNES clerk, almoner to the king, by whom he was presented Mar. 22nd 1358-9 as to the Prebend of Wigginton on account of the custody of the lands and heir of Ralph le Botiller, and Apr. 1st and June 28th 1359 as to the Prebend of Wigginton and Comberford on account of the advowsons of the churches of the inheritance of Sir Philip Marmion (who held them *in capite*) being in the king's hands. After this date we have never again found Comberford associated with Wigginton in the name of this Prebend. On July 1st of the same year Keynes was made the king's keeper of the royal park of Foli-John (or Folyjon) and forester in the cover and bailiwick of Ascot, for which he had 2*d*. a day for life paid by the Constable of Windsor Castle. He died in 1367.

JOHN DE THORP clerk was presented July 4th 1367 to that Prebend which Thomas de Keynes deceased had, whilst he lived, in the *King's Free Chapel of Tamworth*: this being the first time we find the Church thus styled. He was admitted on the 9th of the same month. Moreover he was Parson of Nailstone in the diocese of Lincoln, and had a Prebend in the royal chapel of St. Mary and All Saints, York. He exchanged these three preferments for the Church of Cotenham in the diocese of Ely, with the next.

THOMAS DE OLDYNGTON or HOLDYNGTON had the king's letters of presentation Jan. 18th 1368-9, and was instituted Feb. 7th.

EDMUND DE STAFFORD Lord of Clifton-Campville made an exchange Sept. 26th with the last and received this Prebend Oct. 12th 1387 from the king, who granted him ratification Apr. 9th 1392. He exchanged with Alex. Herle for a Canonry in Exeter Cathedral, and within six or seven weeks the king Mar. 15th 1394-5 gave assent to the Pope's election of him (Jan. 15th) to the See of Exeter. He was Keeper of the Privy Seal, Chancellor of the Exchequer in 1396 and 1401, and died Sept. 3rd 1419, in great repute as "profundus legum doctor."

ALEXANDER HERLE had the king's grant Jan. 24th 1394-5, but almost immediately exchanged for a portion in Norton Church in the Diocese of Durham with the next.

JOHN PROPHETE had the royal presentation Feb. 17th 1394-5, and ratification May 15th following. He was Dean of Hereford from 1393 to 1407, and then of York till his death in 1416, and was also Keeper of the Privy Seal.

JOHN CHAUNDELER clerk was presented Oct. 3rd 1402 on the resignation of the last. From the Deanery of Salisbury he was raised to the Bishopric in 1417, and died July 16th 1426. He soon gave up this Prebend.

JOHN BREMORE clerk was presented July 21st 1404, and died in 1418.

JOHN HUNTE clerk had the royal gift Oct. 26th 1418.

ROBERT SHIRYNTON clerk succeeded Nov. 29th following, and ceased after almost twenty years.

WALTER SHIRYNGTON clerk was presented June 20th 1438, and continued till 1448.

ROGER MERSSHE clerk obtained this Prebend Feb. 3rd 1448-9, which he afterwards exchanged for a Canonry of Windsor with the next.

GILBERT HAYDOCK was presented Aug. 19th 1459.

JOHN DUNMOWE clerk succeeded July 25th 1484 on the death of Haydock. He was made Bishop of Limerick Nov. 13th 1486, but died the king's ambassador at the Papal Court in 1488 before he could visit his See.

JOHN DUNMOWE succeeding his uncle was presented Feb. 3rd 1488-9, and continued till his decease in 1498.

WILLIAM TAILLOUR a king's scholar in the University of Oxford had the Prebend Oct. 2nd 1498, but soon died.

WILLIAM LATHIS or LATHES Bac. Theol. succeeded June 1st 1499.

THOMAS NORBURY chaplain of the royal household followed Mar. 8th 1501-2 on the death of Lathes. He resigned.

BRIAN DARLEY professor of Theology was presented Mar. 29th 1505, and died in 1527.

JOHN GOLDE clerk M.A. almoner to Mary queen of France had the king's gift July 14th 1527.

ROGER DYNGLEY clerk fellow of All Souls College, proctor of the University of Oxford in 1518, and chaplain to Henry VIII came very soon after, and died in 1538.

HUMFREY HORTON clerk presented Aug. 1st 1538, was the last Prebendary.

6. PREBENDARIES OF BONEHILL.

RALPH DE HENGHAM, not Heneham as it seemed to be *(see p.* 17) in the faded and almost illegible inquisition of Mar. 13th 1291.

HENRY DE LYCHFELD was admitted Nov. 22nd 1311.

RICHARD DE WOTTON was presented by Baldwin son of Sir Alexander de Frevile about 1324. He was a Comptroller of the Exchequer in the reigns of Edward II. and Edward III., but lost his sight for more than the last ten years of his life. In 1347 this Prebend was thought to be void and John de Tamworth had a royal grant of it. In a petition to the king and council in Parliament Wotton pleaded his own cause, and gave an account of himself and how he was thus ousted out of his Prebend, praying that as he was now blind, old and feeble it might be given back to him, as a work of charity and for the soul of Baldwin his late lord. The king ratified the Prebend to him Jan. 28th 1347-8.

JOHN DE TAMWORTH Oct. 18th 1347.

PETER DE WOTTON was instituted Mar. 29th 1348. He exchanged for a Canonry of Bangor with the next.

PETER DE GYLDESBURGH clerk was presented Feb. 3rd 1351-2 by the king and admitted May 4th following. In 1364 he gave up to his namesake.

PETER DE GYLDESBURGH clerk had the king's presentation dated Sept. 25th.

JOHN DE NEWENHAM warden of St. Nicholas' Chapel at Stanford in the Diocese of London exchanged with the last, and had this Prebend Feb. 28th 1364-5, after having also received the Church of Fenny Stanton Jan. 29th from the king. He speedily resigned.

THOMAS WEST the younger followed Sept. 17th 1366. He exchanged for a Canonry in St. Mary's of Leicester with his successor here.

NICHOLAS KYNCHALE clerk was presented Nov. 24th 1377. He is mentioned as Rector of Drayton Basset in 1361 and 1368 and of Buckby in 1370. He had ratification in this Prebend June 20th 1390, but ceased soon after by death.

WILLIAM ROK had letters of presentation Oct. 19th 1389, probably by some oversight.

HUGH BUCKENHULL clerk was presented Sept. 27th and admitted Oct. 19th 1390.

THOMAS SCODYER made an exchange with the next.

THOMAS MORTON Warden of the Hospital of Sts. Stephen and Thomas in Romney received this Prebend June 10th 1421. Morton too exchanged the Prebends of Alton Pancras in Salisbury Cathedral and of Bonehill for that of North Newbald in York Cathedral with John Prentice.

JOHN PRENTICE was presented July 14th 1423, and died in 1445.

WALTER BATE resigned in 1479.

ROBERT CRAKE clerk was presented Oct. 28th 1479.

JOHN GEFFREY died in 1493.

THOMAS BIRCHOLD B.C.L. presented Jan. 17th 1493-4 gave up in a few years.

JOHN WYLCOCKS, WILCOKKES, or WYLKOKS M.A. was presented Dec. 15th 1501. He died in 1538.

EDWARD LEIGHTON clerk S.T.B., Fellow of Cardinal College, and Proctor of the University of Oxford in 1524, had the Prebend from Henry VIII. Dec. 11th 1538. Anthony à Wood says that he "did solely give himself up to please the unlimited humour of the king." He resigned.

ROBERT JOHNSON clerk followed. He compounded for first fruits here Dec. 21st 1547, was the last Prebendary of Bonehill, and died in 1559. He was of the University of

Cambridge, was generally esteemed "a learned man,' and in Mary's reign stood up against the teaching of Hooper, Bishop of Gloucester.

The following elections of Churchwardens and Wardens of the Lights and Wardens of St. George's Guild were made at the Leets of the Staffordshire side of the town, except in 1508 when they are entered on the only court-roll for the Warwickshire side which is now to be found between 1460 and 1517.

CHURCHWARDENS.

1456.   Oct. 26th.   John Goldeson and John Geffrey.

1470.   Oct. 23rd.   Pet. Goaboute and John Wolshawe, this year.

1488.   Nov. 4th.   Rich. Wolshawe and Will. Greene elected and sworn.

1505.   Oct. 21st.   Rich. Breten and John Irpe for the next year.

1507.   Oct. 12th.   Rich. Breten, Tho. Goldeson.

1508.   Oct. 16th.   John Gyllot and Nich. Symond.

1509.   Oct. 16th.   John Jekes and John Irpe for the next year.

1511.   Oct. 21st.   Rich. Breten and Rich. Coton for the next year.

Fragmentary roll: date gone.   Tho. Ensor, Will. Wyldy.

WARDENS OF THE LIGHTS: WARDENS OF ST. GEORGE'S GUILD.

1470.   Oct. 23rd.   Tho. Wever Keeper of the Light of St. Nicholas, Bp., and of St. Katherine;
Rob. Gouldson Keeper of the Light of the B. V. Mary and of the Holy Trinity.

1488.   Nov. 4th.   Rob. Shepard for the *Trinite lyght.*
Nich. More for the Light of St. Nicholas.

1505.   Oct. 21st.   Rich. Coton Keeper of the Light of the B. Mary.

      Rich. Clerke Keeper of the Light of St. Nicholas, Bp.

      Tho. Towe Warden of St. George, Martyr.   All three for the next year.

1506.   Oct. 12th.   John Hille Warden of St. George.

      Will. Bowth Keeper of the Light of B. Mary, sworn.

      John Lyssot Keeper of the Light of St. Nicholas.

1508.   Oct. 16th.   Rich. Alcote Warden of St. George.

      John Swypson Warden of St. Nicholas.

      Ralph Smyght Warden of the B. Mary.

1509.   Oct. 16th.   Nich. Bisshoppe Warden of St. George's Light.

      Steph. Barow Keeper of the Light of the B. Mary.

      Rich. Cotton Keeper of the Light of B. Nicholas.

1511.   Oct. 21st.   John Mason Warden of St. George.

      John Grene Keeper of the Light of St. Nicholas.

      Nich. Webster for the Light of the B. Mary.   All three for the following year.

1516.   Oct. 18th.   John Lysot, Tho. Goldson, Wardens of the Guild of St. George.

      John Repyngton Warden of the Light of St. Nicholas.

      Tho. Dorlaston Warden of the Light of the Holy Trinity.

Fragmentary roll: date gone.   Rog. Aschewode of the Staffordshire side Keeper of the Light of St. Nicholas, and there remained 6s. in the box given up to him.

      Nich. Webbestar Keeper of the Light of the Holy Trinity for the next year, and there was 2s. 6d. in the box given up to him.

      Hen. Erpe Keeper of the Light of St. George for the next year, and there was 11s. 6d. in the box given up to him.

Finis.

APPENDIX.

In the course of this work we alluded *in page* 94 to the alliance between the family of Frevile, Lords of Tamworth Castle, and that of Willington which once enjoyed the dignity of the baronial rank. The pedigree of the latter is here given in full: therein are brought together the bounds of nine long centuries in the history of Tamworth, and the age of Ethelfled and St. Edith stands represented in the present generation of this town.

Pedigree of Willington.—*John de Willington*, of Willington, co. Derby, lived at, or immediately after, the time of William the Conqueror, since we find that his son,

Nicholas de Willington, lord of Willington, was contemporaneous with Robert, abbot of Burton, in the reign of King Stephen. He was *s.* by his son,

Nicholas de Willington, lord of Willington. A dau. and heiress of Nicholas de Willington *m.* Hugo de Finderne, from which marriage descends Sir J. H. Crewe, Bart. of Calk Abbey. In Dugdale's *Monasticon*, it appears that both this Nicholas and his father were liberal benefactors to the convent of Repton; and, according to Lysons, the manor and church of Willington were given to the convent by these Willingtons. His brother,

Ralph de Willington, who served under the banner of Richard Cœur de Lion, and was at the siege of Acre, settled at Sandhurst, in Gloucestershire, *temp.* King John, whence the manor-house obtained the name of Willington Court. He afterwards founded St. Mary's Chapel, in the Abbey of St. Peter's, Gloucester, now called "The Ladye Chapel." He *m.* Olympias, dau. and heir of William Franc, grandson and heir of Sir Humphrey Franc, Knt., and was father of

Sir Ralph de Willington, living 37 Henry III, who *m.* Joan, dau. and heir of Sir William Champernowne, of Umberleigh, in Devon. After this marriage, their descendants, as is recorded by Sir William Pole, in his *History of Devon*, left their own arms and took those of Champernowne, omitting the billets, viz., gu., a saltier, vair. Their son,

Sir Ralph de Willington, of Willington Court, co. Gloucester, and of Umberleigh, styled by Risdon, "a worthy warrior," was governor of the castle of Exeter, 38 Henry III, and sheriff of Devon 39th and 42nd of the same reign. He *m.* Juliana, supposed by Sir William Pole to be the dau. and heir of Sir Richard de Lomen, as the lands of Lomen came to their descendants. They had issue,

    I. John de Willington, summoned to parliament as a baron from 3 Edward III to 12th of the same reign, when he *d.*, leaving, by Joan his wife, a son,

       Ralph de Willington, who was also summoned as a baron to parliament 16 Edward III. This Ralph was in the wars of Scotland and France ; he *m.* Eleanor, dau. of John, Lord Mohun, of Dunster, but *d. s. p.* in 1349, when the baronry became extinct.

    II. Reginald (Sir), *d. s. p.* 29 Edward III.
    III. *Henry* (Sir), of whose line we have to treat.
    IV. Thomas, living 22 Edward III.

The 3rd son,

Sir Henry Willington, Knight-banneret, was, with his brother John, made prisoner at Bannockburn, and, subsequently, taking part with the Earl of Lancaster against the Despencers, was executed at Bristol in 1322. He *m.* Margaret, dau. of Sir Alexander Frevill, by Joane his wife, a co-heiress of the Marmions *of Tamworth*, and left a son and successor,

Sir Henry Willington, 23 Edward III. He *m.* Isabel, daughter of Sir John Whalesborow, and had two sons,

    I. *Sir John Willington*, his heir.
    II. *Thomas Willington.*

Sir Henry was *s.* by his eldest son,

Sir John Willington. of Umberleigh, who was present at the coronation of Richard II. He *m.* Matilda, dau. of Sir Walter Carminow, and had issue,

    I. Ralph Willington, of Willington Court, Gloucester, who *d. s. p.* 10 Aug. 1382.
    II. John, of Willington Court, who *d. s. p.* 1397.
    I. *Isabel*, co-heir, aged 25, 5 Henry IV (1404), *m.* William (son of Sir John) Beaumont, of Shirwell, whence descended two heiresses, from one of whom (who *m.* Sir John Bassett) is descended Arthur Bassett, Esq., present owner of Umberleigh, and from the other (who *m.* John Chichester) is descended the baronet family of Chichester and the Marquess of Donegal.
    I. *Margaret*, co-heir, *m.* John, son of Sir John Wrothe.

John Willington (continuator of the male line), by Margery his wife, left a son and successor

William Willington, co. Gloucester, whose will is dated 22 Jan. 1500.

He was father of

John Willington, who had two sons, viz.,

I. *William*, of Barcheston, who, though the principal property had passed to the Beaumonts and Wrothes, inherited considerable estates in the cos. of Gloucester and Warwick, including lands at Brailes, co. Warwick, where his ancestors had held lands from an early period (John Willington. the first baron, and his father, Sir Ralph, both held property there *temp.* Henry III and Edward II). He *m.* Ann, dau. of Richard Littleton, Esq. of Pillaton, co. Stafford, and widow of Thomas Middlemore, Esq. of Edgbaston, by whom he had issue,

1 Margery, *m.* 1st, Thomas Holte, Esq. of Aston; and 2ndly, to Sir Ambrose Cave, Knt., chancellor of the duchy of Lancaster; by her first husband she had a son, Edward Holte, who *m.* Dorothy, dau. of Sir John Ferrers, of Tamworth Castle; and by Sir Ambrose Cave she had an only dau. and heiress, who, marrying Sir Henry Knollys, had two daus. only, one of whom, Elizabeth, *m.* Sir Henry Willoughby, of Risley, and the other, Lettice,. *m* William, 4th Lord Paget, ancestor, by her, of the present Marquess of Anglesey.

2 Godith, *m.* Basil Fielding, Esq. of Newnham, ancestor of the Earls of Denbigh.

3 Elizabeth, *m.* to Edward Boughton, of Lawford.

4 Mary, *m.* to William Sheldon, Esq. of Beoley and Brailes.

5 Margaret, *m.* to Sir Edward Grevill, ancestor of the Earls of Warwick.

6 Ann, *m.* to Francis Mountford, Esq. of Kingshurst.

7 Catherine, *m.* 1st, to Richard Kempe, Esq.; 2ndly, to William, son of Sir Richard Catesby, of Lapworth; and 3rdly, to Anthony, son of Sir George Throckmorton.

II. *Thomas*, of Hurley Hall.

The 2nd son,

Thomas Willington, of Hurley Hall, 32 Henry VIII (1541), *m.* Joan, only dau. of Nicolas Nitingale, Esq., and heiress of her mother, Joyce, who was sister and heiress of John Waldyve. It appears from Sir William Dugdale, in his *History of Warwickshire*, that, after this marriage, the Willingtons, through the marriage of William Waldyve, great-grandfather of Joane, wife of Thomas Willington, with Sibilla, dau. of Simon Bracebridge, became lineally descended from King Egbert, by the marriage of Reynburn, son of Guy, Earl of Warwick, lineal ancestor of the Bracebridges, with Leonetta, dau. of King Athelstan, and hence also collaterally descended from Ethelfleda, who rebuilt Tamworth Castle A.D. 914, she being dau. of King Alfred, and aunt of King Athelstan, and great-granddau. of King Egbert. Editha, also, the patron saint of Tamworth Church, was Athelstan's sister. (*Vide* pedigrees of Willington, Bracebridge, and Saxon Earls of Warwick—Dr. Thomas's edition of *Dugdale's Warwickshire*). By this marriage, Thomas Willington had issue,

I. *Waldyve Willington*, his heir.

II. John Willington, of Whateley, from whom are descended the Willingtons *of Whateley and Tamworth, d.* 8 Aug. 1617; he *m.* Isabel Litherland, and had issue,

Anticle Willington, of Whateley, who had two sons, *Thomas* and *George.* The elder,

Thomas, was father of another Thomas, who, marrying Mary, dau. of John Swynfen, Esq. M.P. for Tamworth, *temp.* Charles II, had a son, Thomas, who. *d. s. p.*, and a dau. and eventual heiress, *Jane*, who *m.* John Skip, Esq. of Ledbury and Whateley, high sheriff for Warwickshire 11 George I, and from that marriage descends John Martin, Esq., late M.P. for Tewkesbury, present owner of the Whateley estate.

George Willington, the younger son of Anticle, was father of Richard, and he of another Richard, whose son, John Willington, of Tamworth, had, besides daus., five sons, viz., John, of the Inner Temple ; Bayley, lieut-gen. in the army, col. commandant of the 2nd battallion of artillery ; Richard ; *Thomas* ; and Francis, rector of Walton-on-Trent; all of whom are now deceased without having left any issue male, excepting Thomas, who had a son, the present Francis Willington, of Tamworth.

Thomas Willington was *s.* by his eldest son,

Waldyve Willington, Esq. of Hurley, who *m.* 1st, Joyce, dau. of George Winter, Esq. of Worthington, co. Leicester ; and 2ndly, in 1563, Margery, sister and co-heir (with her sister, Jane, who *m.* Lionel Skipwith, Esq.) of Michael Bracebridge, Esq., and by her had, besides

Thomas, his heir, two other sons, and a dau., Elizabeth Willington, *m.* to William Aston, son of Sir Walter Aston, of Tixall, and uncle to Walter, 1st Lord Aston, of Forfar.

Waldyve Willington was drowned at Sawley, and bur. 3 Aug. 1569, at Rawlston. His eldest son,

Thomas Willington, Esq. of Hurley, *m.* 9 July, 1599, Alice, dau. of his uncle, John Willington, of Whateley, and had issue, with two younger sons and five daus.,

Waldyve Willington, Esq., his heir, baptised 18 April, 1600. He was an active parliamentarian, and governor of Tamworth Castle, which had fallen into the hands of Cromwell. He *m.* 27 Oct. 1630, Joane Porter, of Edgbaston ; and *d.* in 1676, having two sons and three daughters. His eldest son,

Waldyve Willington, Esq. of Hurley, baptised at Kingsbury, 3 March, 1633 ; *m.* 9 May, 1665, Susannah, dau. of Roger Jones, of Hackney, and had issue,

I. *William*, his heir, *b.* 29 July, 1666 ; *m.* Elizabeth, dau. of Thomas Hood, Esq. of Bardon Park ; but *d. s. p.*

II. *Thomas*, of whom presently.

III. *Waldyve*, of Hurley Hall (whom his brother, William, made his heir), high sheriff for Warwickshire, 13 George I, *b.* 26 Dec. 1677 ; *m.* Martha, dau. of Richard Hervey, Esq. of London, and dying 10 Sept. 1733, left issue,

1 *William*, of Hurley Hall, *d. s. p.* 24 March, 1752, leaving his three sisters co-heiresses, viz.

1 Susannah Willington, *m.* Charles Floyer, Esq. of Hints, whence, from two daus., co-heiresses, are descended the present families of Floyer *of Hints* and Levett *of Wichnor Park*.

2 Catherine, *m.* the Rev. Richard Jackson, M.A. of Tarrington, in Herefordshire, founder of the Jacksonian professorship at Cambridge. She *d. s. p.* in 1762 ; her husband survived until 1782, aged 82, when the estate of his deceased wife went to that lady's cousin, *Thomas Willington*, of whom below.

3 Mary, *d. unm.* in 1762.

Waldyve Willington *d.* 2 Nov. 1677, and was *s.* by his eldest son,

William Willington, Esq., who *d. s. p.*, leaving his youngest brother, Waldyve (of whom we have spoken), his heir. His next brother,

Thomas Willington, *b.* 13 June, 1674, was buried at Kingsbury, April, 1718, leaving two sons, the elder of whom,

Thomas Willington, of Nottingham, marrying Miss Mary Ashe, of Lincolnshire, *d.* in July, 1768, and had issue (besides William, a midshipman, who *d.* young at sea).

Thomas Willington, Esq., who *s.* on the death of the Rev. Richard Jackson, husband of his cousin Catherine, one of the three co-heiresses of Waldyve Willington. He *d.* in 1815, *s. p. Francis Willington*, Esq. of Tamworth, is now male representative of the family (refer back to descendants of John Willington, of Whateley). He was *b.* 10 April 1800, *m.* 16 May, 1825, Jane-Anne, dau. of the late Henry James Pye, Esq. of Faringdon House, Berks., formerly M.P. for that co., and poet-laureate to George III, and has had issue,

I. *Francis Pye*, M.A., Rector of Over Worton, Oxfordsh., *b.* 14 April, 1826, *m.* Mary, eldest daughter of Edward Sherringham, Esq., of Coxford Abbey, Norfolk.
II. Waldyve-Henry, *b.* 2 April, 1831, and *d.* 17 Dec. 1850.
III. John-Ralph, M.A., *b.* 23 April. 1837.
IV. Henry Edward, M.A., *b.* 30 Dec. 1838.

Arms—Gu., a saltier, vair, arg. and az.
Crest—A pine-tree, vert. fructed, or.

MODERN VICARS OF THE CHURCH.

Whilst the last pages of this work were passing through the press, we were solicited to add some account of the Vicars or Ministers who have held this Church since the Reformation. Though it is beyond the scope of our present subject, we give it here, as it will doubtless possess much interest for our readers.

It will be useful first of all to mention the

LAY PATRONS OF THE CHURCH.

1. THE QUEEN, from 1558 to 1581.
2. EDMUND DOWNING and PETER ASHTON, Oct. 27th 1581. *See p.* 55.
3. JOHN MORLEY and ROGER RANT, Feb. 21st 1582-3. *See p.* 56.
4. THOMAS REPINGTON of Amington, Esq., purchased the advowson and patronage of the Vicarage and Church May 10th

1583, as we have stated in *p*. 56. By deed dated Nov. 2nd 1603 made on the marriage of John Repington his son with Margaret daughter of Sir Edward Littleton knt. he settled the advowson (amongst his estates) on them and on their heirs in tail-male. He died Dec. 14th 1615, and next day was buried at Tamworth.

5. SIR JOHN REPINGTON knt. and MARGARET his wife. He died Jan. 23rd 1625-6, and was buried here on the 29th.

6. SIR JOHN REPINGTON knt. son of the last was buried here June 26th 1662.

7. SEBRIGHT REPINGTON, Esq., son of Sir John, died Sept. 18th 1698, and was buried on the 21st in the N. Chancel of this Church.

8. EDWARD REPINGTON, Esq., eldest son of Sebright died Feb. 23rd 1734-5 s.p.m., and was buried on the 26th at Amington Chapel.

9. GILBERT REPINGTON, Esq., half-brother of the last died in Feb. 1738-9, and was buried Mar. 2nd at Tamworth.

10. EDWARD REPINGTON, Esq., succeeded his father Gilbert, and died in Feb. 1759 s.p.

11. CHARLES REPINGTON, Esq., brother of Edward died Dec. 8th 1764.

12. CHARLES EDWARD REPINGTON, Esq., succeeded his father, and dying June 27th 1837 aged 82 years was buried in the N. Chancel of this Church. With him the family of Repington became extinct.

13. EDWARD HENRY A'COURT, Capt. R.N. afterwards Admiral, a second cousin came into the estates of C. E. Repington and took the additional name of Repington. His grandmother Annabella wife of Sir William Pierce Ashe-A'Court bart. was sister of Matilda wife of Charles Repington 11th patron; he died unmarried and was buried in this Church Sept. 22nd 1855.

14. CHARLES HENRY WYNDHAM A'COURT-REPINGTON, Esq., son of Major-General Charles Ashe-A'Court succeeded his uncle and is the present patron of the Church.

NOTES.

The Ecclesiastical Commissioners of Edward VI. in 1548 decreed that there should be a preacher and two other ministers to serve the cure here, the former with a salary of 20*l.* a-year and the latter with 8*l.* a-year each. *See p.* 49. In her charter to the town Oct. 10th 1588 Elizabeth granted to the Guardians and Governors of the Free Grammar School here the appointment of the Preacher and two curates subject to the approval of the High Steward. *See p.* 57. The clashing interests of the Repington family and the Guardians were for some time reconciled by a compromise: it was agreed that as the former had *advocationem, donationem, et liberam dispositionem, et jus patronatûs vicariæ et ecclesiæ de Tamworth,* and the charter of the latter expressly had the word *curates,* the Repingtons should nominate the Vicar, and the Guardians the two assistant ministers. Owing to the insufficiency of the salaries, the alienation of tithes and all the church-property, and other causes it became usual to appoint the same person both to the vicarage and to the two curacies. In later times when a third service was required in the Parish Church, a public subscription was raised to assist the Vicar in providing the stipend of an assistant Curate.

VICARS.

JOHN WRIGHT. Soon after her accession to the throne and at the establishment of the Reformation, queen Elizabeth appointed John Wright to be the minister or preacher. He died in April 1578, and on the 10th was buried here.

ROGER MOLDE was appointed by Elizabeth in 1578. In 1583 he was presented to the Church of Austrey in Warwickshire by Humfrey Ferrers, Esq. on the concession of Robert, Earl of Leicester. Still he resided at Tamworth till 1610 when he resigned and went to Austrey where he died in 1619.

SAMUEL HODGKINSON B.A. was nominated and appointed to the Vicarage Aug. 28th 1610 by John (afterwards Sir John)

Repington and Margaret his wife, and he was to preach here at least once a fortnight. He ceased in the autumn of 1629.

THOMAS BLAKE was born in Staffordshire about the year 1597. He entered Christ Church in the University of Oxford in 1616 but whether in condition of a student or servitor Anthony à Wood did not know, took the degrees of B.A. May 5th 1620 and M.A. Feb. 21st 1622-3, and afterwards "had some petit employment in the church bestowed on him." He was appointed to the Vicarage here Nov. 12th 1629 by Sir John Repington, and the Guardians of the School gave him the office of the two curates so that he became both Vicar and perpetual curate and resided in the College House. In the Parish Register is the entry: "Aprill, 1631 : 27. Mar. Thomas Blake, Minister of Tam., & Jane Wagstaff of Drayton basset." It does not appear that he had any issue.

This clergyman became one of the most celebrated Puritan divines of his day, and wrote some pamphlets and works which stirred up much controversy and brought many into the polemical lists against him, amongst whom were Richard Baxter, Blackwood, Tombes, and Humphries. About the end of March 1644 he quitted Tamworth but without giving up the living here and became pastor of St. Alkmund's in Shrewsbury. When the Presbyterian party began to be dominant he adhered to it, subscribed the Covenant in 1648 amongst the Ministers of Shropshire, and soon showed himself a zealous brother of the cause.

Whilst Mr. Blake was away, Theophilus Lord, M.A. who had been called to be preacher here in Sept. 1643 by the Parliamentary Governor of the town and by the Corporation, took the whole duty of Minister in May following by desire of the Committee of Safety for Warwickshire, and continued till his death. He was buried here Jan. 13th 1649-50. Mr. Blake now returned from Shrewsbury. Being a constant advocate of the Puritan cause he was nominated by the Lord Protector Oliver Cromwell to be one of the assistants to the commissioners of Staffordshire for the ejecting of such whom they called ignorant

and scandalous ministers and schoolmasters.   During the rest
of his life he continued in his pastoral duties here and in the
use of his pen, and died in June 1657 when he was about sixty
years old.   He was buried in this Church on the 11th : at his
funeral (which many ministers and others of the neighbourhood
attended) a sermon was delivered from the pulpit and on the
occasion of his death an oration was made which were afterwards
published under the following title : *Paul's last Farewel, or a
Sermon preached at the Funerall of that Godly and Learned
Minister of Jesus Christ, Mr. Thomas Blake.   By Anthony
Burgesse, Pastor of the Church of Sutton-Coldfield in Warwickshire.   With a Funeral Oration made at Mr. Blakes death by
Samuel Shaw, then Schoolmaster of the Free-School at Tamworth.
London* [March 25] 1658. 4°.   The address *To the Reader* dated
Sutton-Coldfield, Octob. 19, 1657.   The sermon (on Acts xx.
36, 37, 38) chiefly on the duties of the pastoral office occupies
pp. 24, the oration pp. 4.

The works of this eminent divine which we have seen are as
follows.

*The Birth-Priviledge : or, Covenant-Holinesse of Beleevers and
their Issue in the time of the Gospel.   Together with the Right
of Infants to Baptisme.   London.* [March 18th, 1643-4] 1644.
4°. pp. 33.   Dedicated, *To his dearly affected and beloved the
Bailiffes and Burgesses of the ancient Borrough of Tamworth
in the Counties of Stafford and Warwick together with all the
Inhabitants of the said Parish.*

*Infants Baptisme, freed from Antichristianisme.   In a full
repulse given to Mr. Ch. Blackwood, in his assault of that part
of Christ's possession, which he holds in his heritage of Infants.
(Intituled by him) The Storming of Antichrist.   London.*
[Aprill 29th] 1645. 4°. pp. 130.   The second part of this work
at p. 62 is, *A Vindication of the Birth-priviledge, or Covenant-
Holinesse of Believers and their Issue, in the time of the Gospel,*

*Mr. Blakes Answer to Mr. Tombes his Letter.   In Vindica-
tion of the Birth-Priviledge, or Covenant holinesse of Beleevers.
and their Issue, in the time of the Gospel.   Together with the*

right of Infants to Baptisme [with a commendatory preface by *Edm. Calamy* and *Richard Vines.*] *London.* [Aug. 7th] 1646. 4º. pp. 114.

Vindiciæ foederis; or, a Treatise of the Covenant of God entered with Man-kinde, in the several Kindes and Degrees of it, in which the agreement and respective differences of the Covenant of Works, and the Covenant of Grace, of the Old and New Covenant are discust....... Three *Scripture-Texts by Mr. John Tombes in the first part of his Antipœdobaptisme sorely handled, and totally perverted, are fully vindicated.......*[with a recommendatory address by *Richard Vines* and *Sam. Fisher.*] *London* [January 29, 1652] 1653. 4º. pp. 488. The dedication, *From my study in Tamworth, Novemb.* 4. 1652.

The Covenant Sealed. Or, a Treatise of the Sacraments of both Covenants, polemicall and practicall, especially of the Sacraments of the Covenant of Grace....... Together with a brief Answer to Reverend Mr. Baxter's Apology, in defence of the Treatise of the Covenant. *London.* [July 7] 1655. 4º. pp. 668. The dedication, *From my study in Tamworth, Jun.* 5. 1655.

Mr. Humphrey's second Vindication of a Disciplinary Anti-Erastian, Orthodox, Free-admission to the Lords-Supper, taken into Consideration, in a Letter occasionally written by Mr. Blake Pastor of Tamworth, and by a Friend of Truth [S.B.] *made publick. London.* [September 30th] 1656. 4º. pp. 12. Dated at the end, *Tamworth, July* 15.

In the Athenæ Oxonienses is also given a work, *Meditations* called *Living Truths in dying Times,* 1665 [*sic*] in tw., which neither the author or his later editor nor we have found. Anthony à Wood also mentions a *Sermon on Gal.* ii. 15. printed in 1644. 4º.: which he had not seen at Oxford or elsewhere and we cannot discover in London.

SAMUEL LANGLEY.

RALPH ASTLE. On the resignation of Samuel Langley, Sebright Repington Nov. 10th 1662, appointed Ralph Astle, on condition that he exercised the pastoral functions in person and preached at least every fortnight unless unavoidably hindered. He resigned Dec. 16th 1663.

SAMUEL LANGLEY graduated M.A. at Cambridge, being a Fellow of Corpus Christi College there, and then he was invited to Swettenham in Cheshire. Thence he had a call to Tamworth in 1657, being elected Nov. 20th to the offices of preacher, minister, and curates by the Guardians of the School, and on the same day appointed Vicar by Sir John Repington with the obligation of preaching once every Lord's day at least, unless lawfully hindered. He first became resident July 1st following, taking up his abode in Bolehall for all the rest of his life and not in the College House. He gave up the living in Nov. 1662, but when Ralph Astle surrendered the cure was re-appointed Dec. 17th 1663 by Sebright Repington on condition of preaching every fortnight, and he continued incumbent till his death Jan. 20th 1693-4 aged 72 years. On the 23rd he was buried in the N. Chancel of this Church. His tombstone has lately disappeared; but it recorded that he was, son of Thomas the excellent minister of Middlewich in Cheshire, brother of Thomas fellow and ornament of Jesus College Cambridge, father of Thomas vicar of Kingsbury, and husband of Sarah for forty-four years : and it added that " til within 4 years of his deceas he was never hindred from preaching in course twice every Lord's day so elaborately as to inform the learned in difficult texts, and yet edify the meanest." He is mentioned in terms of commendation in the Memoirs of William Whiston the well-known Arian divine : whilst he was Rector of Swettenham he wrote the following work on Excommunication.

Suspension Reviewed, stated, cleered and setled upon plain Scripture-Proof, agreeable to the former and late Constitutions of the Protestant Church of England and other Reformed Churches. ......Together with a Discourse concerning private Baptisme, inserted in the Epistle Dedicatory. By Samuel Langley, R.S. in the County Palatine of Chester. London [May] 1658. 8°. pp. 222. The dedication dated *Decemb.* 15. 1657.

SAMUEL COLLINS of Clare Hall Cambridge graduated as B.A. in 1673 and as M.A. in 1677. He was presented to the

Rectory of Willoughby-Waterless in Leicestershire by Thomas earl of Stamford, and was admitted Jan. 2nd 1683-4. Without resigning that living he was appointed Vicar of Tamworth June 19th 1694 by Sebright Repington; and Aug. 1st following, the Guardians of the School granted him the two curates' places, which the High Steward confirmed. He was collated Sept. 19th 1705 to the Prebend of Gaia Minor in Lichfield Cathedral; and dying in Oct. 1710 was buried on the 16th at Tamworth.

GEORGE ANTROBUS of Clare Hall, Cambridge, became B.A. in 1702 and M.A. in 1706. He was presented by Queen Anne to the Church of Kingsbury in Warwickshire being admitted Jan 21st 1706-7. Edward Repington appointed him Vicar of Tamworth Jan. 8th 1710-1. He received the stipends of the Vicar and Curates and inhabited the house appropriated to the Minister. Dying in 1724 he was buried Aug. 4th in this Churchyard close to the S. Porch.

ROBERT WILSON was of Brasenose College Oxford, and took the degrees of B.A. Apr. 20th 1710 and M.A. June 25th 1712. Whilst he was beneficed at Thorpe-Constantine in Staffordshire, Edward Repington bestowed the Vicarage of Tamworth upon him Dec. 29th 1724, and he held it on the same terms as those to whom he succeeded. He was appointed July 3rd 1742 to the Prebend of Lytton, Bath and Wells; and dying at Tamworth Nov. 30 1758 was buried Dec. 5th here.

SIMON COLLINS of Magdalen Hall Oxford passed B.A. May 10th 1744 and M.A. Nov. 14th 1747. He obtained the headmastership of the Free Grammar School of Tamworth Oct. 26th 1752 by appointment of the Guardians and Governors. When the vacancy of the Vicarage was shortly expected through the ill-health of Mr. Wilson the Guardians determined to bring to a legal determination their claim to the exclusive right of presentation; and the day after the incumbent's death they elected Simon Collins (Dec. 1st 1758) "as preacher or minister and curates," with all profits and stipends belonging to the offices; and they confirmed this appointment Jan 5th following. In the course of a few months Charles Repington made his appointment in the person of William Sawrey, who immediately began legal proceedings to oust his opponent. At the summer assizes at Stafford in 1761, a verdict was given in favour of the Repington family to the total exclusion of the Guardians, and in October of that year Mr. Collins had to resign. He continued to be Schoolmaster till his demise in 1793.

WILLIAM SAWREY of Queen's College Oxford became B.A. Mar. 1st 1725-6 and M.A. May 18th 1727. He was appointed Master of the Free Grammar School here Feb. 8th 1732-3, and continued for about eight years. On Dec. 26th 1745 he was inducted into the Rectory of Elford. Charles Repington granted him May 5th 1759 the Vicarage of Tamworth with the curacy, and appointed him to be vicar of the vicarage and curate of the curacy for his life upon the terms that he should reside here and preach in the Church at least once a fortnight. He obtained possession of the incumbency in October 1761 and held it together with Elford till his death in 1792.

MICHAEL BAXTER of the University of Dublin graduated as B.A. in spring 1779 and commenced M.A. in summer 1782. He became Vicar here by the appointment of Charles Edward Repington, but died within a few years.

FRANCIS BLICK, of St. John's College, Oxford, B.A. June 17th 1774 and M.A. Apr. 11th 1777, was for some time Curate of Sutton Coldfield. He was chosen Vicar of Tamworth in 1796 by Charles Edward Repington, and continued for forty-four years. He was moreover Rector of Walton-with-Rolleston in Staffordshire and of Wisseth in Suffolk; and Nov. 7th 1828 he was collated to the Prebend of Pipa Parva in Lichfield Cathedral. He died Apr. 3rd 1842, in the 88th year of his age, and was buried in this Churchyard.

ROBERT CHAPMAN SAVAGE of St. John's College Cambridge, B.A. 1835 M.A. 1840, was raised from the curacy to the Vicarage here in 1842 by Capt. Edward Hen. A'Court. In 1845 he was presented by the Queen to the Vicarage of Nuneaton, which he still enjoys.

EDWARD HARSTON, of Clare College Cambridge, B.A. 1834 and M.A. 1837, was Rector of St. Stephen's, Ipswich for ten years before he came to Tamworth. He was presented to this Church as Vicar in 1845 by Capt. Edward Henry A'Court, and continued here till 1854 when the Crown gave him the Vicarage of Sherborne, Dorset. He resigned that living on account of ill-health in 1868, and was appointed by Lord Hylton in 1870 to the Rectory of Holcombe near Bath.

JOHN MOULD, of St. John's College, Cambridge, graduated as B.A. in 1838 and as M.A. in 1841. He was incumbent of St. Paul's, Walsall and Master of the Grammar School there in 1844, and Master of Appleby Grammar School in Leicestershire from 1845 to 1854. In this year he was presented to the Vicarage of Tamworth by Admiral Edward Henry A'Court-Repington. He resigned in 1865 on being appointed Vicar of Oakham-with-Egleton and still enjoys that living.

JAMES OGILVY MILLAR, of Christ's College, Cambridge, graduated as B.A. in 1849, and commenced M.A. in 1852 and LLD. in 1864. He was Curate of South Petherton, Somersetshire from 1851 to 1853, and of Cirencester from 1853 to 1855; then Assistant Minister of St. John's, Edinburgh from 1855 to 1860; and Perpetual Curate of Elson, Hants, from 1860 to 1865. C. H. W. A'Court-Repington, Esq. appointed him Vicar of Tamworth in 1865, and he became Rural Dean, as were also his two predecessors. He held this living till 1869, when he received his present preferment to the Vicarage and Rural Deanery of Cirencester.

RICHARD RAWLE, late Fellow and Assistant Tutor of Trinity College, Cambridge, B.A. 1835 M.A. 1838, was Rector of Cheadle in Staffordshire 1839; Principal of Codrington College, Barbados 1847; Vicar of Felmersham near Bedford 1867; and in 1869 was presented by C. H. W. A'Court-Repington, Esq. to the Vicarage of Tamworth which he now holds.

✠

INDEX.

NOTES.

Page 87, line 11. The Comberford Monument has been again built up and hidden from sight since we wrote our account of it.

Page 104, line 2. It now seems certain that we were right in believing that William Pountfreyt did not take the Deanery in 1403-4. For it was as Dean of Tamworth that John Bernard in 1418 sued John Gresbrook of Middleton husband-man for a debt of 20*l*.

Page 109, line 10. Sir Baldwin Frevile alleged that the presentation of 1334 being made before the composition was not included in it, so that the turn of 1342 as the *first* fell to him. But for the Crown it was answered, that the presenta-tion of 1334 (which stirred up all the debate) was the *first one* of the agreement; and besides it would be unjust for the Freviles to enjoy two presentations to the one each of the other parties. The words of the agreement of 1334 "q'd p'd'ca Joh'na de Frevill in ista p'ma vacaco'e p'sentet," show how groundless was such a plea on Sir Baldwin's part. The cause came on in Easter term 1343, and judgment for the Crown was given at the following Trinity.

CORRECTIONS.

Page 21, line 3, *for* proparty *read* pourparty.
   ,, 32, ,, last *and* p. 33 l. 7, *for* Grent *read* Grene.
   ,, 63, ,, 3, *for* a W. window *read* an E. window.
   ,, 79, ,, 4, *for* Alice *read* Matilda.
   ,, 113, ,, 22, *for* All Saints *read* Holy Angels.